This book is the first guide to Berg's second opera, *Lulu*, written in non-technical language and intended for those students and music lovers wishing to become familiar with one of the masterpieces of twentieth-century music. Jarman presents a clear and concise introduction to the musical language and to the intricate musical and dramatic structure of Berg's opera. The volume also examines the literary background, the genesis, composition, and performance history. The volume also includes source documents and critical responses to the opera, as well as photographs from the première and from recent productions, a synopsis, bibliography and discography.

Cambridge Opera Handbooks

Alban Berg
Lulu

CAMBRIDGE OPERA HANDBOOKS

Published titles

Richard Wagner: *Parsifal* by Lucy Beckett
W. A. Mozart: *Don Giovanni* by Julian Rushton
C. W. von Gluck: *Orfeo* by Patricia Howard
Igor Stravinsky: *The Rake's Progress* by Paul Griffiths
Leoš Janáček: *Kát'a Kabanová* by John Tyrrell
Giuseppe Verdi: *Falstaff* by James A. Hepokoski
Benjamin Britten: *Peter Grimes* by Philip Brett
Giacomo Puccini: *Tosca* by Mosco Carner
Benjamin Britten: *The Turn of the Screw* by Patricia Howard
Richard Strauss: *Der Rosenkavalier* by Alan Jefferson
Claudio Monteverdi: *Orfeo* by John Whenham
Giacomo Puccini: *La bohème* by Arthur Groos and Roger Parker
Giuseppe Verdi: *Otello* by James A. Hepokoski
Benjamin Britten: *Death in Venice* by Donald Mitchell
W. A. Mozart: *Die Entführung aus dem Serail* by Thomas Bauman
W. A. Mozart: *Le nozze di Figaro* by Tim Carter
Hector Berlioz: *Les Troyens* by Ian Kemp
Claude Debussy: *Pelléas et Mélisande* by Roger Nichols and Richard
   Langham Smith
Alban Berg: *Wozzeck* by Douglas Jarman
Richard Strauss: *Arabella* by Kenneth Birkin
Richard Strauss: *Elektra* by Derrick Puffett
Richard Strauss: *Salome* by Derrick Puffett
Kurt Weill: *The Threepenny Opera* by Stephen Hinton

Alban Berg
Lulu

DOUGLAS JARMAN
*Principal Lecturer, Department of Academic Studies
Royal Northern College of Music, Manchester*

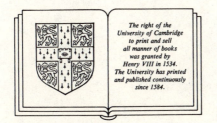

The right of the
University of Cambridge
to print and sell
all manner of books
was granted by
Henry VIII in 1534.
The University has printed
and published continuously
since 1584.

CAMBRIDGE UNIVERSITY PRESS

*Cambridge
New York   Port Chester   Melbourne   Sydney*

Published by the Press Syndicate of the University of Cambridge
The Pitt Building, Trumpington Street, Cambridge CB2 1RP
40 West 20th Street, New York, NY 10011, USA
10 Stamford Road, Oakleigh, Melbourne 3166, Australia

First published 1991

Printed in Great Britain at the University Press, Cambridge

British Library cataloguing in publication data

Alban Berg: Lulu. – (Cambridge opera handbooks).
1. Opera in German. Berg, Alban, 1885–1935
I. Title
782.1092

Library of Congress cataloguing in publication data

Jarman, Douglas.
Alban Berg, Lulu / Douglas Jarman.
   p.   cm. – (Cambridge opera handbooks)
Discography.
Includes bibliographical references.
ISBN 0 521 24150 2. – ISBN 0 521 28480 5 (pbk.)
1. Berg, Alban, 1885–1935. Lulu. I. Title. II. Series.
ML410.B47J28   1991
782.1 – dc20   90–1637 CIP MN

ISBN 0 521 24150 2 hardback
ISBN 0 521 28480 5 paperback

To Jan and Albert

Contents

Illustrations

General preface

This is a series of studies of individual operas written for the opera-goer or record-collector as well as the student or scholar. Each volume has three main concerns: historical, analytical and interpretative. There is a detailed description of the genesis of each work and of the collaboration between librettist and composer. A synopsis considers the opera as a structure of musical and dramatic effects, and there is also a musical analysis of a section of the score. The analysis, like the history, shades naturally into interpretation: by a careful combination of new essays and excerpts from classic statements the editors of the handbooks show how critical writing about the opera, like the production and performance, can direct or distort appreciation of its structural elements. A final section of documents gives a select bibliography, a discography, and guides to other sources. Each book is published in both hard covers and as a paperback.

Acknowledgments

Like the *Wozzeck* volume in this series, the present book began life as a collaboration between myself and the distinguished American composer and scholar George Perle. Although the pressure of Professor Perle's other commitments eventually forced him to withdraw from the venture, anyone familiar with his writings on *Lulu* will realise the extent to which I am indebted to his work.

I am grateful to the Director of the Musiksammlung of the Austrian National Library in Vienna, Hofrat Gunter Brosche; to Dr Nicholas Chadwick, the Assistant Music Librarian, and Miss C. M. Hall of the British Library; to Universal Edition (Alfred A. Kalmus), Universal Edition Vienna and its archivist Dr Elisabeth Knessl; the Directors of the Alban Berg Stiftung and to Mr Anthony Hodges, Librarian of the Royal Northern College of Music, Manchester.

My thanks are also due to Reg Wilson, Katherine Wilkinson and the Royal Opera House, Covent Garden; to Daniel Cande, Catherine Heuls and the Paris Opéra; to Eric Thorburn and the Scottish Opera; and to Chantal Huys and the Théâtre de la Monnaie, Brussels.

My especial thanks are due to Dr Celia Skrine who translated the first three documents in the final section of the book.

1 *Introduction: chronology and background*

Berg seems to have become acquainted with *Earth Spirit*, the first of Frank Wedekind's two *Lulu* plays, in the early 1900s when he was nineteen years old. Frida Semler, a young American girl who was the daughter of a business acquaintance of Berg's brother Charley in New York, spent the summers of 1903 and 1904 as a paying guest at the Bergs' country residency, the Berghof on the Ossiachersee, and remembers copies of Schnitzler's *Reigen* and Wedekind's *Earth Spirit* being read by the younger members of the family at that time.[1]

It is not perhaps surprising that Berg should have been familiar at so early an age with the work of an author who was still unrecognized by the literary establishment, for a devotion to new art of all kinds was something of a fashion with the young people of the period. In his autobiography *The World of Yesterday* Berg's Viennese contemporary Stefan Zweig has described the passion for art and literature that seized him and his class-mates in their mid-teens, a passion 'to discover the latest, the newest, the most extravagant, the unusual which had not yet been dwelt upon at length, particularly by the official literary circles of our daily newspaper':

We were the vanguard and shock troops of every sort of new art merely because it was new, merely because it wished to change the world for us, whose turn had now come to live our lives.

For Zweig, as for Berg, Wedekind was one of the touchstones of this fashionable literary sensitivity:

Wherever an experiment was attempted, perhaps a Wedekind production or the reading of some new lyrics, we were on the spot with all the powers not only of our souls but with that of our hands as well.[2]

One such experimental production took place in the spring of 1905 when the great satirist and writer Karl Kraus (himself still a

1

young man of thirty-one) produced the second of Wedekind's two *Lulu* plays, the recently published *Pandora's Box*, in a private club performance in the Trianon theatre in Vienna on 29 May. The part of Lulu in this production was played by Wedekind's future wife Tilly Newes, while Wedekind himself played the role of Jack the Ripper. Kraus took the small part of the negro Kungu-Poti, one of Lulu's clients in the final scene, and delivered a lecture on the play before the performance. Sitting in the sixth row of the small theatre was the twenty-year-old Alban Berg.

Berg's early contact with the *Lulu* plays, at a crucial stage in his personal development, generated an enthusiasm for Wedekind that was to stay with him for the rest of his life. The extent to which the performance at the Trianon theatre gripped the young Berg's imagination can be judged by the fact that he was still deeply affected by and writing enthusiastic letters about the play some two years later. In November 1907, for example, he wrote to Frida Semler describing Wedekind as 'the really new direction – the emphasis on the sensual in modern art' and commenting that

at last we have realized that sensuality is not a weakness, not a surrender-ing to one's own desires but an immense strength – the centre of all our being and thought ... only through an understanding of the sensual, through a profound insight into the depths – or rather, perhaps, the heights – of mankind can one arrive at a true idea of the human psyche.[3]

In a letter written six months later to his future wife Helene, Berg cites Ibsen, Wedekind, Altenberg, Strauss and Pfitzner as examples of great men whose 'sublime ideas' spring from their belief in love.[4] Berg's views on the stature of the two composers in this list may have changed in his later years, but his devotion to Altenberg, Ibsen and Wedekind never wavered.

Karl Kraus' lecture, a translation of which is given in the documentary section of this book, had an equally permanent impact on the young Berg. Kraus was, in any case, one of his literary heroes and, like a large part of the population of Vienna, Berg was a devoted reader of Kraus' satirical periodical *Die Fackel*. Twenty years after the Trianon performance, when Berg came to set *Pandora's Box*, his views of the *Lulu* plays were still deeply influenced by the views expressed by Kraus in this lecture. When in April 1934 Berg sent his congratulations on the occasion of Kraus' sixtieth birthday, his greetings took the form of a quotation of the music and text of some bars from Act II of *Lulu* – the setting of the words 'A soul who, from the other side, rubs the sleep from its eyes.' They were the words with which Kraus had begun his 1905 lecture in the Trianon theatre.

In 1926, with the triumphant Berlin première of *Wozzeck* behind him, Berg began to look around for a play on which to base the libretto of a new opera. Various plays were considered and rejected until eventually the choice was narrowed to two possibilities: Gerhart Hauptmann's *Und Pippa tanzt*, in which Berg had been interested for some time, and the two *Lulu* plays of Frank Wedekind. Unable to make up his mind, Berg sought the advice of his friends and colleagues, many of whom (like his wife Helene) tried to persuade him that Hauptmann's was a better and more suitable play than the Wedekind.

By late 1927 Berg seemed to have finally decided on *Pippa*, and the following January, when he was staying with Alma Mahler in Portofino, he met Hauptmann in Rapallo to discuss the financial arrangements. By March 1928 Berg was already making sketches for the music and engaged on arranging the libretto: 'Naturally', he wrote to Schoenberg on 30 March, 'I'll have to make great cuts in Hauptmann's drama to suit my purpose, indeed I even intend to combine the third and fourth (last) acts, thereby somewhat alleviating the weakness of precisely that portion of the drama.'[5]

A month later he was beginning to have doubts about the project. Hauptmann and his publishers were insisting on what Berg called 'extraordinarily oppressive conditions – a fifty per cent share of the royalties, another twenty per cent of the libretto and five per cent of the music'[6] – while refusing to give Berg exclusive rights to the work: 'It will probably be *Pippa*', wrote Berg to Schoenberg on 26 April, 1928, 'though Hauptmann's oppressive conditions ... don't make the work seem very advisable – from the "practical" standpoint.'[7] When it became clear that neither Hauptmann nor his publishers were willing to reconsider their unrealistic terms, Berg turned again to the *Lulu* plays. Negotiations were started with Wedekind's widow in autumn 1928 and completed almost a year later in July 1929, when Berg wrote to his publishers, Universal Edition, announcing that 'our action and my obstinacy in the *Lulu* affair have been crowned with success'. By this time, however, Berg, anticipating a successful outcome, had already started work on the opera.

The chronology of the early stages of Berg's work on *Lulu* is somewhat puzzling. In the official catalogue of the Berg manuscript holdings in the Austrian National Library Dr Rosemary Hilmar describes a large (double-page) row-chart which shows the derivation from the Basic Set of some of the subsidiary sets employed in the work. This chart, which is reproduced in Plate 1 is, according to Dr Hilmar's catalogue, dated 17 July 1927,[8] a date that suggests that Berg drew up the chart before negotiations with Wedekind's widow were even begun, let alone completed.[9] There also exists an early sketch for the opening bars of the Prologue, dated 23 June 1928, which shows that, by then, Berg already had many of the basic musical ideas of the opera clear in his mind. This early attempt at the Prologue was abandoned; and Berg, leaving the Prologue to the end, began work on the opera proper. As a letter to Schoenberg reveals, most of the first scene of the work had been completed by September 1928 – still, that is, before agreement had been reached with Frau Wedekind.

Work on *Lulu* continued, on and off, during the winter and spring of 1928/9 despite frequent interruptions, most notably those caused by Berg's attending the revival of *Wozzeck* at the Berlin Staatsoper in October 1928 and his involvement in the preparation for the Oldenburg première of *Wozzeck* the following March. *Lulu* was then put aside, however, and Berg devoted most of the summer of 1929 to the composition of the concert aria *Der Wein*, a work commissioned for the Czechoslovakian soprano Růžena Herlinger.

It was unusual for Berg to accept commissions and he did so on only two occasions, both of which necessitated his putting aside work on *Lulu*. We may perhaps wonder at his willingness to stop work on what was, after all, the major undertaking of these final years, and there is some evidence to suggest that the composition of both *Der Wein* and the Violin Concerto fulfilled some personal psychological need. Equally important, however, is the fact that both commissions came at a time when they also met more practical needs. In the case of the Violin Concerto the commission came when, his music banned by the Nazis and the lucrative royalties from performances of *Wozzeck* having stopped, Berg's financial position made it difficult for him to refuse. In the case of *Der Wein*, work on the aria undoubtedly provided a convenient opportunity to explore specific technical problems posed by the work on *Lulu*.

On 20 September 1929, less than two months after completing *Der Wein* and while still working on the full score of the piece, Berg wrote to Webern announcing his discovery of 'a good solution to the problem of using rows for such a lengthy work. (Apart from the different forms which I have long since already derived from them.)'[10] The origin of this new 'solution' was his work on *Der Wein*. Before composing the Aria, Berg had confined himself, in *Lulu*, to using subsidiary note-rows that could be derived from the Basic Set by overlapping various segments; after, and partly as a result of his work on the Aria, he arrived at a quite new series of note-rows, derived by extracting notes from the Basic Set according to a consistent pattern. He then went back and integrated these new rows – which were to become the source of much of the most important musical material of the later sections – into the already composed sections of the opera.

During the winter of 1929/30 Berg was involved with the preparations for a number of productions of *Wozzeck* (including the Vienna première in March 1930) and also of the first complete performance of the Three Orchestral Pieces op. 6 at Oldenburg in April 1930, and it was not until July that he was able to leave Vienna for his retreat at the Berghof in Carinthia and return to his work on *Lulu*. By this time, although he was still working on the first act, the shape of the piece as a whole was fixed. He was able, on 7 August, to send Schoenberg a diagrammatic sketch of the shape of the opera, a sketch which, although later modified in various details, shows that the overall structure was already clear to him. The Sonata movement, which is the chief formal component of the first act, was sketched out in the summer of 1930, and the act was finally completed in July 1931.

'A run of adversities' – family difficulties, a serious accident to his wife Helene and his own ill health (including his recovering from an attack by a swarm of wasps) – made it 'difficult to find the quiet and concentration necessary for work on the opera' during the summer of 1932.[11] From that point onwards, however, work on *Lulu* began to move more swiftly, aided in part by Berg's realization that *Wozzeck* could now make its own way in the world and no longer required his attendance at all rehearsals, and also by the purchase, in November 1932, of his own country retreat at the Waldhaus in Carinthia where he could withdraw and devote himself entirely to work.

By September 1933, after a summer spent working at the Waldhaus, Berg was able to tell Webern that Act II was finally finished. He was now, he reported, able to embark on 'the most difficult part – Act III',[12] a task which, staying at the Waldhaus over winter, he began in January 1934 and which progressed steadily during the early months of the year. His letters to his wife over this period reveal that at the beginning of March he was working on Lulu's encounter with her second client ('I'd much rather [write to you] than get Alwa killed by the negro', he wrote to Helene on 4 March).[13] A few days later (9 March) he was working on one of Countess Geschwitz's solos (whether the one that immediately comes after Alwa's death or the later 'Nocturno' is not clear) that follows. Finally, having completed Act III, Berg returned to the Prologue, and by 6 May the Prologue, and with it the whole of the opera, was completed in short score.

Although the National Socialists did not come to power in Germany until January 1933, they were a major political force both in Germany and to a certain extent in Austria also, from 1928 onwards. Already in 1928 the Austrian National Socialist party had attempted to stop the Vienna production of Krenek's *Jonny spielt auf* declaring that the work represented the 'Jewish-negro defilement' of the State Opera by 'a Czechoslovakian half-Jew'.[14] The day before the 1930 Vienna première of *Wozzeck* the official newspaper of the Austrian Nazi party had published an article denouncing the opera as 'one of the most provocative agit-prop pieces ever written', and calling on the Viennese public to give 'this unspeakable botched work' and the 'compromising Austro-Marxist activities of the State Theatre the answer they deserve'.[15] By 1932 many of the theatres that had been going to perform *Wozzeck* had withdrawn and, as he wrote to Erich Kleiber, Berg began to be aware of his increasingly difficult financial situation 'now that so many theatres don't dare to perform *Wozzeck*'.[16] By January 1934, when he was working on Act III, there was a real possibility that it might no longer be possible to perform *Lulu* in an Austrian or a German theatre. Kleiber, who hoped to give the first performance of *Lulu* – having already given the première of *Wozzeck* – wrote to Berg in April 1934 to express both his belief in the composer (despite his obvious puzzlement and dismay that Berg should have chosen such a subject) and his misgivings about the chances of staging the piece in Berlin:

I don't know how it will be with the opera in Berlin. Having read the libretto, however, I must tell you that enormous obstacles will stand in the way and I hope that you won't take it amiss if I confess that having read this final version I can't really think how you have composed it . . . If, mainly because of the libretto, the piece should encounter difficulties in Berlin I will fight for it with all my strength and, should the performance be obstructed, you have my promise that I will rehearse and conduct the work wherever you want . . . Perhaps there is a way to moderate the final scenes in the music . . . I had myself imagined the libretto in a much milder form . . . but there are secret ways that have nothing to do with us interpreters and you yourself will best know why you felt that you had to set this text . . . We know that you will have a lot, and much that is powerful, to say to us and we await it impatiently.[17]

Berg had originally anticipated a scandalous première with some glee ('When this new opera is produced in the Germany of today there'll be an outburst of the most colossal indignation' he had written to Kleiber in April 1933) and, even now, seemed unable to regard the opera's not being performed as a real possibility. 'You ask me where you could produce *Lulu* if Berlin (and therefore all Germany) refuse it', he replied to Kleiber's letter, 'we'll discuss that later. Perhaps we shall never need to ask the question – I hope not.'[18] Not until May did he finally become convinced that a German première was impossible:

The die is cast [wrote Berg to Kleiber on 29 May], I've just had a letter from Furtwängler to say that 'in view of the gravity of the situation' it is quite out of the question that *Lulu* should be accepted for the present anywhere in Germany. Yet he knows (and others know) that I am a German composer and an Aryan, just as Wedekind is a German and an Aryan.[19]

In the same letter Berg told Kleiber of the plan that he had already suggested to his publishers, Universal Edition, of making an orchestral suite from the opera: 'U.E. will publish it as soon as they can so that every orchestra (in the world!) can play it this autumn. Would you, could you, and are you brave enough to give the first of all these performances?'[20]

Although Berg had completed the opera, he had as yet only written the work in short score. He now began to work on the orchestral score, starting with those sections which he wanted to include in the suite – the Rondo, the 'Film Music' Ostinato Interlude and the *'Lied der Lulu'* from Act II, and the Variation Interlude and final Adagio from Act III. The manuscript of the *Lulu* suite was sent off to his publishers by August 1934. It was for long thought that the manuscript of these *Symphonic Pieces from 'Lulu'* was lost; in fact, as the article reprinted in the documentary section of this book makes clear, the manuscript was returned to Berg who, to save time and effort, simply dismantled it and absorbed the different movements of the suite into the full score of the opera at the relevant points. Having completed the suite Berg then went back to the beginning of the opera and began to orchestrate the piece chronologically, starting with the Prologue.

True to his promise, and with characteristic bravery, Kleiber gave the first performance of the *Lulu* suite in Berlin on 30 November 1934. An undisputed success, according to the *Prager Tageblatt*, it was to be the last time that Berg's music was performed in Germany for ten years. Four days later Kleiber resigned his post as General Music Director of the State Opera.

The première of the *Lulu* suite came at a time when the relationships between musicians and the Reich had reached a critical point. A few days earlier Furtwängler, who had already protested about the Nazi policy towards Jewish musicians, had published a spirited defence of Hindemith and had been greeted with an ovation at a performance of *Tristan* that he conducted that same evening. On 7 December 1934, three days after Kleiber's resignation, Goebbels publicly attacked Hindemith and the atonal composers in a speech at the Berlin Sportsplatz, declaring that atonality 'furnished the most dramatic proof of how strongly the Jewish intellectual infection had taken hold of the national body'.[21] A few days after Goebbels' speech the periodical *Die Musik*, which had become the official organ of the Nazi Cultural Committee, observed of the press reception of the *Symphonic Pieces*:

It is significant that one of the most degraded foreign yellow newspapers, the *Neue Wiener Journal*, was able to quote several Berlin reviews which seemed favourably inclined to the music of this emigré Jewish musician . . . such reviews are inadmissible in our age of directed public opinion, for they befuddle the mind and hinder the rebuilding of our culture.[22]

In January or February 1935 Berg was approached by the young American violinist Louis Krasner who wanted to commission him to write a violin concerto. Initially surprised by the idea, Berg finally agreed. Starting work on the concerto in March, Berg devoted the early summer to the composition of the piece, completing the short score on 15 July.

Meanwhile, there remained the matter of the opera's première to be dealt with. Following the original Berlin performance, the *Lulu* suite had been played with considerable success abroad – in Prague, Geneva, Brussels, London and Boston – and, now that a German première was impossible and an Austrian première unlikely, Berg was eager to negotiate with those foreign houses that might stage the opera itself. The Budapest State Opera had already expressed an interest and in July Berg wrote to the Hungarian composer Sándor Jemnitz, to tell him that '*Lulu* should be ready for performance in the coming 1935/6 season. The score and piano score will be ready after the end of the year. Nothing is definite yet about the première – for the time being there are serious negotiations with the Americans and Prague (Deutsches Theater).'[23]

But there were financial as well as artistic considerations to be taken into account, for Berg's material worries were becoming increasingly desperate:

If it depended on my artistic knowledge and human feelings alone [wrote Berg to Kleiber], I would have happily telegraphed you 'please première *Lulu* Prague, second half of the 1935/6 season' but it isn't as easy as that. Apart from it demanding the greatest effort from me (there are still about 400 pages of the score to complete), from Stein (the piano score) and from the publishers (material), to make sure that the opera is performable within the year (all of which is natural) the financial question plays the most important role at the moment. As with *Wozzeck* in its time, the publishers expect a large sum of money, such that hardly three or four European theatres can be considered, in order to make it possible to print the piano score and produce the material. And the 'rake off' that I get from the première must also take into account that I'm already deeply in debt to the publishers. I won't trouble you with my financial worries but believe me, if I shrink back from the worst extreme of selling off (below cost) the Waldhaus (my workshop) it is only because I expect a 'rake off' from the première. How badly I need it is proved by my accepting a commission for a violin concerto, which meant that I had to stop work on the instrumentation of *Lulu* for four or five months. The publishers expect this rake off from an American première and have already been negotiating for a long time with different places in the USA. Up to now everything is quite without guarantee. Do you think that such a poorly endowed theatre as the Deutsche Oper in Prague could even approximately rival an American financially?[24]

By now Berg was at a low point physically, as well as in terms of morale. Berg's first biographer Willi Reich, and all subsequent writers, have dated the beginning of Berg's final illness from mid-August when he received an insect sting which gradually led to septicaemia. But there is considerable evidence to suggest that Berg was ill before this incident. He was certainly ill when working on the Violin Concerto in the summer of 1935, as we know not only from a letter to Webern in which he complained of 'never feeling wholly well – asthmatic, with a nervous heart and deadly tired'[25] but also from the description which Helene Berg gave to Louis Krasner of how 'Alban, ill in bed and tortured with pain, worked frantically and without interruption to conclude the composition of the Violin Concerto. Refusing to stop for food or sleep he drove his hand relentlessly and in fever: "I must continue," Berg responded to his wife's pleading, "I cannot stop, I don't have the time." '[26] It seems likely, however, that Berg had been ill and in considerable pain for at least a year, and perhaps longer, before his death. Reich recounts how 'large doses of aspirin, which he had been taking secretly for weeks, kept Berg on his feet in the last two months of his life'.[27] But Leonard Marker, who studied composition with Berg from 1929 onwards, remembers 'the innumerable bottles of aspirin – a thousand to a bottle – that Berg took daily and that we [Reich and Marker] had to deliver to him'.[28] The fatal insect sting entered a body that was already weakened, and Berg – ill, exhausted by work on the Concerto, demoralized, depressed and desperately worried about his financial situation – was in no condition to fight the infection. The boils that resulted from the sting were, as Webern later realized, less the cause of Berg's final illness than a symptom of his already precarious state of health.[29]

From late August onwards Berg's whole physical constitution seems to have broken down, and he was plagued by a series of ailments – boils, from which he had been suffering for months, continuing trouble with his teeth and gums, blisters and abscess. Despite the constant pain which he was to suffer from this point onwards, Berg returned to the score of *Lulu* and continued work on the instrumentation. 'Das mein Lebensabend. Die Pest im Haus' ('This the evening of my life. The plague in my own home') he wryly observed, quoting from Act II of the opera, in a letter to his publishers on 21 August. 'I groan with Dr Schön, and summoning up all my will power I carry on scoring *Lulu*.'[30] A planned trip to Prague in early September, where the *Lulu* suite was to be performed at the ISCM Festival (International Society for Contemporary Music Festival), had to be abandoned. By mid-October Berg had finished scoring Act II of the opera, and he started work on Act III; but decided to return to Vienna, in early November, in order to be on hand well in advance of the Vienna première of the *Lulu* suite under Kabasta. In the first week of December, when Berg was involved in preparations for the performance of the *Lulu* suite, further boils appeared. Although complaining about the pain, he attended all the rehearsals.

The Vienna première of the suite, with Lillie Claus as the soloist, took place on 11 December in a concert that also included Liszt's First Piano Concerto and Tchaikovsky's Fourth Symphony; it was the first time that Berg had heard a live performance of any of *Lulu* and it was the last time he was to hear any of his own music. After the performance Berg went to celebrate with a few close friends, including Webern and Paul Pisk. Pisk, who was seeing Berg for the last time, remembers how 'although he made several pertinent remarks concerning the vicissitudes of the performance and the attitude of the audience, he looked pale and very ill'.[31] Three days after the *Lulu* suite performance Berg managed to go through the piano score of the Violin Concerto with Rita Kurzmann. He was in great pain, however, and the effort took his last reserves of strength.

On Monday, 16 December a boil that had appeared at the base of his spine suddenly subsided and a fever set in. The following day he was taken to the Rudolfspital. Two days later, although weak after a blood-transfusion, Berg seemed somewhat better. Webern, who had been visiting regularly, later reported to Schoenberg that he 'really had a lot of confidence . . . one could genuinely believe that the matter would pass'.[32] On the evening of Sunday, 22 December, however, Berg suffered a heart-attack and it was clear that the end was near.

I was at the hospital early on Monday 23rd [reported Webern]. I was with Alban for the last time at 5.30 in the afternoon. Since Sunday afternoon the condition had, until then, remained much the same. Yet still we hoped. I had to leave on 26 December for Barcelona, for the Jury of the IGNM contemporary music festival . . . and the last words we exchanged were about my journey. 'I must say goodbye to you', he said. 'You are going on a long journey.' I replied that we would see one another again and that I would come in the morning. 'How nice; how lovely', he said; that was the last thing he said to me. When at about 10 o'clock the doctor, Dr Hoess, was there I spoke to him myself. He had given up hope. The heart was finished . . . I stayed in the hospital until about midnight. I had to leave the room, but there was nothing more to be done.[33]

2 From play to libretto

Frank Wedekind, the author of the *Lulu* plays, was born in Hanover on 24 July 1864, the second of six children born to Dr Friedrich Wilhelm and Emilie Wedekind. Wedekind's parents had met and married two years earlier in San Francisco where his father, having fled Germany after the 1848 Revolution, was practising as a doctor. Their second child was christened Benjamin Franklin after the American president; Friedrich and Emilie were fond of such gestures – their next son was, similarly, christened Wilhelm Lincoln.

In 1884 the twenty-year-old Wedekind left Switzerland, where the family was then living, to study at the University of Munich, and it was here, in a city that was one of the centres of the European avant-garde of the day, that he first became deeply involved in literature and the theatre. Following a break with his father in October 1886 Wedekind, now forced to earn his own living, returned to Switzerland and found work as a journalist on the *Neue Zürcher Zeitung*. He then became publicity manager to the stock cube manufacturers Maggi, the first of a number of unusual and colourful occupations that later included his working in Paris from 1891–4 as secretary to both a travelling circus company (work that perhaps inspired the circus background of the Prologue to *Earth Spirit*) and to the art forger Willy Gretor. It was during these four years that Wedekind visited London, six years after the Whitechapel murders, the series of murders of prostitutes by the never-identified Jack the Ripper on which he was to draw for the final scene of the *Lulu* plays.

Returning to Germany at the beginning of 1895, Wedekind went first to Berlin and then to Munich, where he eventually settled, earning a name for himself as a contributor to the satirical periodical *Simplicissimus*. From its founding in 1896 until its enforced closure in 1933, *Simplicissimus* was one of the most influential periodicals in Germany, and the outlet for a host of talented contributors including Thomas and Heinrich Mann, Hoffmannsthal, Rilke and Schnitzler. From 1901 onwards Wedekind was also one of the leading performers at the famous Munich cabaret *Die elf Scharfrichter* ('The Eleven Executioners') where he read and, accompanying himself on the guitar, sang his own settings of his poems. Berg was later to incorporate the melody of one of these cabaret songs into the last act of *Lulu*.

Wedekind came from a musical family. Before her marriage his mother had earned a living as a singer and actress and his younger sister Erika later became well known as a coloratura soprano. As a schoolboy he had learned the guitar and the flute and, later, the violin, piano and mandolin. Wedekind's cabaret style appears to have been idiosyncratic but effective. Heinrich Mann remembered how Wedekind, thick set and with close cropped hair, would sing in a 'nasal, sharp, cutting voice' with expressive pauses during which he would turn, stooping, to look at the audience. 'Who', asked Mann, 'could grasp the meaning of these songs or of those eyes?'[1] In one of his earliest published pieces Brecht (who set up his own cabaret *Die rote Ziebe* in Munich in 1922) described Wedekind's performance thus:

Whether it was an auditorium he was entering, where there were hundreds of noisy students, or a room or the stage, with his peculiar gait, his sharply-cut, iron cranium, tilted forward – somewhat awkwardly and disturbing – everything suddenly became still ... A few weeks ago he sang in the Bonbonnière with his guitar – those songs – with a brittle voice, somewhat monotonous and untrained. Never has a singer so moved and inspired.[2]

Brecht's own first appearance in Berlin was singing in cabaret to his own guitar accompaniment in a style which he deliberately modelled on that of Wedekind.

Wedekind's appearances at 'The Eleven Executioners' not only gave him a small regular income at a time when he was still dependent on the financial help of his sister Erika, but also, and equally importantly, at a time when his plays were still almost unknown, they gave him an opportunity to present his material to an audience. Wedekind had been writing poems and stories since the age of fifteen. His first major play, *Spring's Awakening*, had been written in 1890 and published the following year, and the original version of the *Lulu* plays was written between 1892 and 1894. The earliest production of one of his plays did not, however, take place until 1898 when *Earth Spirit* (without the Prologue, which was added later) was performed in Leipzig. Wedekind himself took the part of Dr Schön, playing the role 'with a highly stylized mode of acting, devoid of any psychological consistency . . . outrageously wooden in his movements and grotesquely exaggerated in his speech'.[3]

Although neither the Leipzig nor the following Munich performance achieved great success or attracted much attention, the political scandal which erupted on the eve of the Munich première was the beginning of a notoriety that was to follow Wedekind throughout his career. Warned that he was about to be arrested for a political satire published in *Simplicissimus*, Wedekind fled to Zurich. A year later he returned from his self-imposed exile, gave himself up to the police and stood trial. As Franz Schoenberner, the then editor of *Simplicissimus*, later observed

When in 1898 Thomas Theodor Heine and Frank Wedekind, because of a joint contribution, were accused of *lèse-majesté, Simplicissimus* once and for all established its political reputation. The trial at which both artists were sentenced to some months' internment in a fortress was the best publicity stunt a publisher could imagine. Heine, in a sardonic mood, sometimes pretended that the owner of the publishing house, Albert Langen, had intentionally avoided destroying some revealing letters which, seized by the police, served as material for the public prosecutor. It is indicative of the political atmosphere of this time that the whole German intelligentsia reacted against this judgment by a petition for pardon, addressed to the Kaiser himself, and signed by the leading representatives of German art, literature and science. The special issue celebrating the fiftieth anniversary of the journal proudly displayed congratulatory messages from Emile Zola, Leo Tolstoy, Auguste Rodin, Henrik Ibsen, Bjornstjerne Bjornson, Georg Brandes, Edvard Grieg, Constantin Meunier, Fridtjof Nansen and other international celebrities.[4]

By making Wedekind the centre of both widespread admiration and vilification the case elevated him to 'the stature of a symbolic figure'.[5] His subsequent success as a playwright, which began with Max Reinhardt's Berlin production of *Earth Spirit* in 1902 and the 1906 production of *Spring's Awakening* and which culminated in the Wedekind cycle mounted by the Munich Kammerspiele to celebrate his fiftieth birthday in 1914, only served to focus the attack. The shocked public and the political, religious and literary establishment saw Wedekind as an arch-pornographer, a dangerous, immoral and unpatriotic writer who was destroying human values and undermining the ethics of the Reich. To the artistic avant-garde and the anti-establishment factions, on the other hand,

Wedekind was now a heroic figure; a theatrical innovator who, in the words of the critic Friedrich Kayssler, had 'strangled the naturalistic monster called probability'[6] and had dared to confront the true nature of sexuality and of a repressive, inhibited society. Thomas Mann was to call him 'one of the foremost moralists of the continent'.[7] Wedekind's scandalous reputation was to dog him for the rest of his career and, up to 1918 at least, to make his work the subject of constant official censorship.

The original version of what was to become the two *Lulu* dramas was a single five-act play entitled *Die Büchse der Pandora: eine Monstertragödie* ('Pandora's Box: a tragedy of monsters') which Wedekind wrote in his Paris years between the end of 1892 and the summer of 1894. The play was submitted to Albert Langen, the publisher of *Simplicissimus*, in 1895, but was not published. Instead, in the same year, Wedekind began the first of a series of revisions, producing a new four-act play, *Earth Spirit*, by shortening the first three acts of the *Monstertragödie* and inserting a new fourth act (the backstage theatre scene of Berg's Act I, scene 3) between the original second and third acts. This version of *Earth Spirit* – still without the Prologue – was published by Langen in 1895. The Prologue was written for the tenth performance of the play in Leipzig in 1898 and was first published separately in the journal *Die Insel* in 1901. In 1902 a revised version of the remaining two acts of the *Monstertragödie* with a newly written first act was published in *Die Insel*. In 1903, following the successful Reinhardt production in Berlin the previous year, a second edition of *Earth Spirit*, which this time included the Prologue, was published by Langen under the title '*Lulu: Dramatic Poem in Two Parts. Part I: Earth Spirit*'.

By 1903 the two plays had thus, in most important respects, reached the form in which we now know them. Following the Circus Prologue, in which the Animal Trainer invites the audience to step inside his menagerie, Act I of *Earth Spirit* opens with Lulu married to the medical specialist Dr Göll, a marriage arranged by her guardian and lover Dr Schön who wants to be free to marry 'a respectable young lady'. When both this and, in Act II, the subsequently arranged marriage to the painter Schwarz end with the deaths of her husbands, Schön finds Lulu a job as a dancer in a cabaret theatre in the hope that she will there meet another prospective husband. Threatened in Act III with her leaving Berlin with Prince Escerny, an admirer who wants to take her to Africa with him, Schön at last recognizes that he is unable to sever his ties with Lulu. The fourth act of *Earth Spirit* opens with Schön and Lulu now married and their home being used as a rendezvous for her various admirers – the old beggar Schigolch, Rodrigo Quast, an athlete, Hugenberg, a schoolboy, and the lesbian Countess Geschwitz. Overhearing his own son Alwa declare his love for Lulu, the disgusted Schön is finally unable to stand any more, hands Lulu a revolver and tries to persuade her to kill herself. Instead Lulu shoots Schön, and the curtain comes down as the police arrive to arrest her.

In the year that elapses between the last act of *Earth Spirit* and the first act of *Pandora's Box* Lulu has been tried, sentenced and jailed for the murder of Dr Schön. Act I of *Pandora's Box* begins at the point at which Lulu's admirers are about to put into operation a plan for her escape. When she is free, Lulu and Alwa flee from Berlin to Paris. Act II takes place in a Paris casino where, surrounded by an unsavoury collection of representatives of the *demi-monde*, Lulu is being blackmailed by the Marquis Casti-Piani who threatens to reveal her identity to the police. Lulu, Alwa and Schigolch, followed later by Countess Geschwitz, again flee, this time to London where Lulu is forced to earn a living as a prostitute. During the course of the final scene Lulu returns with four clients, one of whom kills Alwa in an argument. The last client is Jack the Ripper who murders both Lulu and the Countess.

The only important subsequent change in the text of the two plays was the translation into German of some passages in the Paris casino scene and the final London scene which had first been in French and English respectively – the encounter between Lulu and Jack, for example, originally took place entirely in a rather idiosyncratic English. These passages were translated into German for the fourth edition of 1911, and the definitive texts were finally published in the *Gesammelte Werke* of 1913.

Figure 1 attempts to summarize the most important of the differences between the various versions of the plays and to show how they relate to the structure of the opera.

In 1904 the *Die Insel* version of the second play was published as a book by Bruno Cassirer with the title *Pandora's Box; A Tragedy in Three Acts* and received its first performance on 1 February 1904 at the Intimes Theater in Nuremberg. Five months later, on 23 July, the book was seized by the public prosecutor, and the author and publisher brought to court on a charge of disseminating

WEDEKIND

1894
PANDORA'S BOX
A Monster Tragedy
in Five Acts

I
II } 1895
EARTH SPIRIT
A Tragedy

III

1902
PANDORA'S BOX
A Tragedy
in Three Acts

IV
V

1898
Prologue

I   The Painter's studio
II Home of Lulu and the Painter
III A theatre dressing room

IV Dr Schön's home

I   Dr Schön's home
II A casino in Paris
III An attic in London

LULU
Opera in Three Acts

BERG

Prologue
ACT I
scene 1
scene 2
scene 3
ACT II
scene 1
Film music
scene 2
ACT III
scene 1
scene 2

Fig. 1   The chronology and development of the Wedekind plays and Berg's opera

obscene material. The book eventually went before three courts, the first two of which, disagreeing on the moral and artistic merit of the play, found respectively for and against Wedekind. In the judgment of the court finding against Wedekind, part of which is reproduced as Document 2 at the end of this book, the 'technical competence of the drama' was a question that could be left open since no artistic merit would be 'enough to remove from its overall effect the sense of repugnance and revulsion'. The second act, in particular, said the court, submitted the reader to 'a quite inexhaustible flow of sexual filth' so that anyone whose 'perception of propriety and impropriety in sexual matters' was that 'prevailing amongst the vast majority of the German people as a whole' would be offended by having 'been caused to feel disgust, revulsion and nausea'. A third court reached a compromise, agreeing that the author and publisher should be discharged while the book itself should be suppressed and all copies destroyed. Wedekind and Cassirer immediately published a revised third edition in 1906, which included a newly written foreword and prologue in defence of the work (see Document 3 below) but performances of the play remained forbidden in Germany by court order. Private performances, such as that which Berg saw in 1905, were still possible in Vienna (even though the Austrian authorities had banned the play as being obscene) but no performances could be staged in Germany, however, until censorship was abolished in 1918 after the war.

By the late 1920s, when Berg began work on the opera, the two Wedekind plays were no longer banned as obscene and were frequently performed, often with some of the greatest actors of the time – Gertrud Eysoldt, Tilly Wedekind, Elizabeth Bergner, Werner Krauss, Fritz Kortner and Emil Jannings all appeared in productions of the *Lulu* plays during this period. But if by this time Wedekind's plays were no longer censored or performed only in heavily cut versions (as was *Spring's Awakening* before 1918), they were, nonetheless, still regarded as shocking and immoral by religious organisations and a large part of the population. In deciding to turn the Wedekind plays into an opera, Berg was, therefore, making a deliberately provocative choice – as many of his friends realized – although in 1928, with a Nazi government in Germany still five years away, neither Berg nor his friends could have predicted just how provocative his choice of text would prove. The plays still, almost a century later, sit uncomfortably in the theatrical repertoire and retain their ability to shock. Perhaps, as Adorno[8] and others have suggested, the unwillingness of the inheritors of the Berg estate to see Act III of *Lulu* completed sprang, at least in part, from a desire to protect Berg's posthumous image – what Karl Neumann wryly called censorship exercised for 'the posthumous protection of a composer from his self-chosen libretto, namely for the protection of Berg from Wedekind'.[9]

By choosing *Lulu*, Berg was also revealing – as he had done earlier in his choice of Büchner's *Woyzeck* – his awareness of and sensitivity to the literary and artistic thought of the period. To the Expressionist playwrights at the turn of the century, when Berg first read the play, Wedekind's importance lay in his being the first author to break with the naturalism of the 1890s – the naturalism of, for example, such writers as Hauptmann, whose *Und Pippa tanzt* Berg almost set instead of *Lulu*.

Set in a precisely defined historical period, Wedekind's two *Lulu* plays seem, at first, to be naturalistic works with a sense of concrete, objective reality – their characters eat, drink, smoke and talk of everyday topics in banal colloquial terms, and there are constant references to the 'modern' world of newspaper offices, of casinos and the Stock Exchange, of the electric doorbell and the telephone. The apparent naturalism of the setting, however, is contradicted by the unreality and illogicality of many aspects of the plays. The plot consists of a series of events that are so grotesquely melodramatic and so obviously contrived (the fleeing from Paris to London apparently engineered only so that Lulu can be murdered by Jack the Ripper or the plan by which Lulu escapes from prison, for example) as to be unbelievable; the dialogue, with its profusion of *non-sequitur*s, inconsistencies and mysteriously recurring sentences, is stilted and deliberately unrealistic; the dramatic method is a disconcerting mixture of the horrific and the farcical. As Neumann has said:

It was the slightly older Wedekind who provided them [the Expressionists] with a powerful poetic method by the unprecedented violence of his new dramaturgy – by his grotesque exaggerations and simplifications . . . by his 'fantastic' style in which hints of mysterious symbolism combine with broad buffoon and circus tricks to produce the most baffling and horrifying effects.[10]

Yet Wedekind was as potent a source of inspiration to those artists (Piscator, Brecht, Grosz, Dix, Weill, Eisler etc.) after the first war who, rejecting the subjectivity, psychology, introspection and élitism of the Expressionists, set out to create an objective, emotionally cool, un-elitist, and politically and socially conscious art. To these artists of the 'Neue Sachlichkeit' ('New Objectivity') Wedekind – with his strange, uncommunicating dialogue, his 'complete indifference to the psychological state of mind' of characters whose 'personalities have little or no basis in reality and whose distortions are not the product of psychological tensions'[11] – pointed the way forward to epic theatre. I shall discuss Berg's relation to the 'new opera' and the Brechtian 'epic' theatre in chapter 8.

In turning Wedekind's *Lulu* plays into an opera libretto, Berg had to overcome two main problems, both of which he clearly identified in his letter to Schoenberg on 7 August 1930, when he spoke of the 'difficulties of cutting four fifths of the Wedekind original' and of preserving 'Wedekind's idiosyncratic language', a language which, as Gittleman observes 'exists nowhere else except in the mouths of Wedekind's characters' and that they 'rarely use for the purpose it was intended – communication'.[12]

Various shortened versions of the *Lulu* plays, aimed at turning the two into a single drama that could be performed in a single evening, had already been made by Erich Engel, Friedrich Sebrecht and, most successfully, by Otto Falkenberg for a production in Munich in 1928, the year in which Berg himself began work on the opera. Although the annotated copies of the Wedekind plays in Berg's personal library show that he worked from the editions published by Müller in Munich in 1920–1, it seems likely that Berg had some knowledge of Falkenberg's version. It is perhaps significant, for example, that like Berg's opera Falkenberg's production used film sequences 'to bridge the numerous scene changes'.[13]

Rather than preparing a complete libretto before starting work on the opera, Berg arranged the text as he went along (as we learn from the letter of 7 August to Schoenberg quoted above in which Berg apologizes for not being able to send a copy of the text 'because finalizing the text goes hand in hand with composing')[14] relying on his knowledge of the main outlines of the piece which, he told Schoenberg, had 'been entirely clear for a long time'.

In some cases his ideas about both the musical and dramatic details changed as the opera developed. Thus, for example, the decision to remove the names of all but the main characters in the work – to omit, that is, the names of Wedekind's Dr Göll, Schwarz,

Prince Escerny, Rodrigo, Hugenberg and many of the subsidiary characters in the last act and to call them simply the 'Medical Specialist', the 'Painter' and so on – was taken only after Berg's work was well advanced; the early sections of the Particell show the names still intact. Similarly, while the decision to double various roles – a decision crucial to the dramatic and musical structure of the work, the effects of which will be discussed in greater detail in chapter 5 – was taken at a very early stage, Berg's ideas about how this doubling was to be effected changed considerably during the course of composition. Indeed, the precise nature of the doubling remains, even in the final manuscript, unclear in at least one detail, since both existing copies of Berg's dramatis personae[15] contain an inaccuracy. One of these dramatis personae (that from the fair copy of the Prologue, which is now in the possession of the British Library) is reproduced as Plate 2 in this book. According to both copies the roles of 'The Theatre Director (Act I), the Police Commissioner (Act II) and the Banker (Act III)' are to be played by a single performer. But this triple role is both physically impossible (since the Police Commissioner does not appear in Act II, as Berg states, but in Act III, scene 1, and does so only a few moments after the Banker has made his final exit) and musically illogical. As we shall see, when, elsewhere in the opera, the same musical material is associated with more than one character it is so because the two (or, in some cases, three) characters are played by the same performer. Since the Banker shares musical material with the Medical Specialist in Act I the role should, if the musical treatment of the other roles is to make sense, be played by the same performer who played the role of the Medical Specialist. Unfortunately, if adopted, the musically logical doubling of the roles of the Medical Specialist and the Banker introduces a new problem because the person playing the Medical Specialist also reappears as the First Client in Act III, scene 2; the return of the same performer in the role of the Banker seriously undermines the dramatic effectiveness of his appearance as the client in the final scene. It seems likely that Berg only gradually became aware of, and because of his premature death never fully solved, the problematic nature of this multiple role.

One other pairing of roles which might also, at first sight, seem dramatically and musically inconsistent – the doubling of the roles of the Animal Trainer in the Prologue and the Athlete – has its origin in Berg's decision to change Alwa's profession. In Wedekind's *Earth Spirit* Alwa is identified as a writer – the author, it is revealed in *Pandora's Box*, of *Earth Spirit* itself. In Berg's *Lulu* Alwa is a composer. 'One could write an interesting opera about this', muses Alwa in Act I, scene 3 and as he does so the orchestra quotes the opening chords of *Wozzeck*, thus specifically identifying the composer Alwa as Alban Berg himself. Similar references to or quotations from Berg's works appear throughout *Lulu*. When, for example, in Act I, scene 2 Schigolch asks Lulu for money, the chromatic instrumental lines associated with this character throughout the opera contrive to accompany his request with a C major chord, the chord that appeared in *Wozzeck* as a symbol of the prosaic nature of money; when in Act II, scene 1 Alwa protests that he is 'only flesh and blood', (words which, by coincidence, occur in both the Büchner and Wedekind texts), he does so to the same melodic line to which Wozzeck sang these same words in the earlier opera; when Alwa uses musical terms to describe the attractions of Lulu, he chooses those terms which form the headings of the movements of Berg's own *Lyric Suite*. Berg had incorporated some similar autobiographical references in the libretto of *Wozzeck*, but the autobiographical references in *Lulu* are both more numerous and more central to the main concerns of the piece, for one of the main concerns of the opera is the opera itself. The opera we are watching is the opera which Alwa considers writing in Act I, scene 3, and it should therefore be Alwa who doubles the role of the Animal Trainer and introduces us to the animals in his menagerie. But, as George Perle has pointed out,[16] such a doubling is impractical since the first words heard as the curtain rises on Act I, scene 1 are Alwa's 'May I come in?' The role of the Animal Trainer is thus doubled by the singer taking the part of the Athlete, the other circus performer in the cast. Throughout the Prologue, however, the Animal Trainer is identified musically as Alwa: it is Alwa's music that he sings and Alwa, alone amongst the chief characters, is not identified as one of the animals in the menagerie.

For the most part Berg confined himself to trimming Wedekind's text (getting rid of the more discursive passages of dialogue, cutting one of the four clients in Wedekind's final scene and omitting some of the subsidiary elements in the Paris scene), ensuring that the arrangement of the final text produced the verbal equivalent of the kind of musical forms he had in mind and adding some directions to clarify the stage action. As the detailed synopsis of the complete three-act opera in the following chapter demonstrates, Berg made no major cuts or changes to Wedekind's plot. Although a few minor elements in Wedekind's story disappear (we hear nothing in the opera of the Schoolboy's attempted suicide, for example, nor – although we assume it must have been successful – are we ever told the outcome of Schigolch's plan to kill the Athlete) Berg's libretto is, as Karl Neumann has observed, 'a remarkable artistic achievement that has earned him unqualified praise even from purely literary circles'.[17]

3 *Synopsis*

Although the formal structure of the opera is discussed in chapter 5, the main formal units are indicated in square brackets in the following synopsis; units that are part of the one musical form dominating each act are indicated in capital letters and bold type. In some cases Berg forgot to give titles to numbers, an oversight that he would doubtless have corrected had he lived to prepare the score for publication; in such cases I have added titles of my own (derived from Berg's own sketches) and have indicated their editorial source with an asterisk.

ACT I

Prologue

A fanfare-like introductory gesture on the orchestra announces the appearance of the Animal Trainer. Accompanied by a clown carrying a bass drum and cymbals, he comes in front of the curtain and invites the audience to step inside and see his menagerie: real wild animals, he promises, not tame domesticated ones like those sitting down in the stalls of the opera theatre. He lists the animals in his menageries (each of which is identified musically as one of the characters in the opera itself) before calling to a stage-hand to bring on the snake.

A cymbal-clash and drum-stroke from the clown, followed by the first statement of the music which is consistently associated with her entrances, introduce the appearance of Lulu who, dressed in the pierrot costume of the first scene, is carried on to the stage. 'She was created to cause mischief, to attract, to seduce, poison and murder,' comments the Animal Trainer fondly, 'sweet innocence – my greatest treasure.'

The stage-hand carries Lulu off again and, accompanied by a

retrograde version of the music that began the Prologue, the Animal Trainer once more invites us to step inside the menagerie as the curtain opens on the first scene of the opera itself.

SCENE 1. *A spacious, but shabbily furnished, studio*

[*Recitative*]

Watched by Dr Schön, the chief editor of an influential newspaper, the Painter is painting a portrait of Lulu as Pierrot. Alwa Schön, a composer, arrives to take his father to the dress rehearsal of his new ballet. Alwa pays his respects to Lulu and enquires after her husband, the Medical Specialist. Pausing to make some critical comments about the Painter's portrait, Dr Schön leaves with his son.

[*Introduction*]

Left alone with Lulu, the Painter stops work and begins to make advances to her. She avoids him and,

[*Canon*]

pausing only to bolt the door, he chases her around the room. The Painter catches Lulu (the canonic vocal lines get progressively closer and eventually coincide), and together they sink on to an ottoman.

[*Coda*]

'I love you, Nelly', declares the Painter kissing Lulu's hands. When she protests that her name is Lulu, not Nelly, the Painter declares that he will, in any case, call her Eva.

[*Melodrama*]

Lulu's husband, the Medical Specialist, is heard banging on the locked door. Lulu and the Painter jump up from the ottoman as the door gives way. Furious and gasping for breath the Medical Specialist advances to strike them with his raised walking-stick but suffers a sudden heart-attack and collapses dead at their feet. Unsure of what to do, the Painter goes to ring for a doctor.

[*Canzonetta*]

Alone, Lulu kneels over the body and – to a voluptuous saxophone melody (that will return at the death of each of her victims) and an equally important dance-like figuration – she tries, half in hope, to persuade the Medical Specialist to come to life again.

[*Recitative*]
The Painter returns. Shocked by what he regards as Lulu's callous behaviour

[*Duet*]
he questions her as to whether she believes in anything, is capable of speaking the truth or has ever really loved. To all his questions Lulu replies that she does not know.

[*Arioso*]
Lulu leaves to change out of her pierrot costume and the Painter voices his fears about what the future holds.

INTERLUDE

The curtain closes as Lulu returns to ask the Painter's help in fastening the hooks on her dress, and the music of the earlier *Canzonetta* and of the *Canon* (now as a three- rather than a two-part canon) is developed by the orchestra.

SCENE 2. *A very elegant salon*

Lulu and the Painter are now married (a marriage, as becomes clear, arranged and financially supported by Dr Schön). In a spoken conversation they discuss the morning's post which has just arrived. Amongst the post are two letters: one from a Parisian art dealer telling the Painter, to his evident delight, of the sale of one of his paintings; the other, to Lulu's obvious displeasure, announcing the engagement of Dr Schön.

[*Duettino*]
The Painter compliments Lulu on her appearance and remarks on his fortune at being married to her: 'Every day it is as though I saw you for the first time . . . I've become completely lost to myself and everything else since I've had you.' They are interrupted by the ringing of the doorbell which Lulu tries, unsuccessfully, to per-suade the Painter to ignore. Returning from answering the door,

the Painter goes to his studio to work, asking Lulu to deal with the old beggar on the doorstep.

[*Chamber Music I for wind nonet)*
The beggar proves to be Schigolch, an old acquaintance of Lulu's. Eager to hear how his 'little Lulu' is doing, Schigolch admires her home and enquires about her new situation. Lulu is touched by his calling her Lulu; 'I have not been called Lulu in the memory of man', she observes. Their reminiscences are interrupted by the ringing of the doorbell and Schigolch leaves as Dr Schön arrives.

[SONATA MOVEMENT]

[*EXPOSITION: First subject*]
'I wouldn't allow that creature into my house', says Schön, referring to the departing Schigolch, whom he believes to be Lulu's father, before turning to the purpose of his visit, which is to demand that Lulu stop seeing him. Schön's opening words coincide with the first statement of the first subject of the Sonata Movement which dominates Act I.

[*EXPOSITION: Transition*]
Schön comments scathingly on the Painter's apparent lack of awareness about his wife's behaviour, observing that since he, Schön, has arranged the marriage and is supporting the Painter's career the least he can expect in return is that her husband exercise some control over his wife. 'He is aware of nothing, neither me or himself', Lulu replies. 'He is blind to such things.'

[*EXPOSITION: Second subject – Gavotte and Musette*]
Schön makes it clear that he wishes to end his acquaintance with Lulu because he wants to marry a respectable young lady. 'I want to be able to bring my bride back to a clean, unsullied home.' Here, as in the first scene of *Wozzeck*, the antiquated dance-rhythms are employed as an ironic comment on Schön's desire for conventional bourgeois respectability. 'But we can still meet', suggests Lulu. 'No', replies Schön to a return of the powerful first-subject theme, 'We shall never meet again anywhere.'

[*EXPOSITION: Coda*]
Above the intense and poignant Mahlerian Lento theme of the Sonata Coda (a theme that symbolizes both Lulu's love for Schön

and the fatal weakness that makes him unable to sever his ties with her), Lulu voices her indebtedness to Schön: 'You took me by the hand, you gave me food and clothing . . . do you think that I can forget such things?' On its reappearances during the course of the opera, the Coda theme will gradually acquire powerful, and in the final scene of Act III, disturbing associations.

[*FIRST SONATA REPRISE: First subject*]
Schön renews his demands that Lulu end her association with him.

[*FIRST REPRISE: Transition*]
'I'd hope that with a healthy young man as husband you would finally be satisfied', declares Schön,

[*FIRST REPRISE: Second subject*]
'I *am* going to be married.' 'What objection can I have?' replies Lulu. 'Do you think that I am jealous of the child?'

[*FIRST REPRISE: Coda*]
The sound of their quarrel has disturbed the Painter who now comes to find out what is happening. 'I must finally have my hands free', mutters Schön to himself as he determines to take the Painter in hand. The music of the Coda reprise is cut off as Lulu leaves.

[*Monoritmica*]
Alone with the Painter, Schön demands that he exercise more control over his wife. Dominated by a persistent rhythmic pattern, the music gradually accelerates. As Schön tells him about Lulu's past and her upbringing, the Painter, distraught and shocked by Schön's revelations, realizes that everything Lulu has told him has been a lie. He dashes away, ostensibly to talk to Lulu – in reality to cut his throat. Lulu re-enters. As the groans of the dying Painter are heard, and as Schön suddenly realizes what has happened, Alwa arrives. Together Schön and Alwa break down the kitchen door and discover the Painter's body. Having reached a climax, the music now begins a long ritardando. Dr Schön telephones the police to report the suicide. The doorbell announces the arrival of the police and, as Schön goes to answer it, Lulu wipes away a spot of the Painter's blood on Schön's hand. 'You will marry me yet', she remarks.

INTERLUDE

[*FIRST SONATA REPRISE: Coda*]
The reprise of the Sonata Coda is picked up at the point at which it was interrupted by the *Monoritmica* and is extended to form the orchestral interlude. At the end the *Grave* interlude music gives away to the sound of an off-stage jazz band as the curtain rises on

SCENE 3. A dressing room in a theatre

Behind a screen Lulu is changing for her performance in the cabaret theatre where she is appearing as a dancer. She asks Alwa if his father is in the audience and announces the imminent arrival of an admirer, a prince who wants to marry her and take her with him to Africa; after all, says Lulu, Dr Schön only put her on the stage in order that she might meet someone rich enough to marry her. She leaves to go on-stage and Alwa, alone, muses momentarily about the possibility of writing an opera about these events. He rejects the idea because the plot would be too absurd to be believable.

[*Choral Variations*]
The Prince, Lulu's admirer, enters but his conversation with Alwa is interrupted by the ringing of an alarm bell.

[*Ragtime*]
The door opens and Lulu rushes in surrounded by a bevy of attendants. She has seen Dr Schön and his fiancée in the theatre audience and has pretended to have a fainting fit so as not to dance in front of them.

[*Sextet*]
Dr Schön arrives, furious, and attempts to force her back on stage. The Theatre Manager agrees to allow her five minutes to recover. Everyone leaves, apart from Schön.

[*SONATA: DEVELOPMENT SECTION*]
Alone with Lulu, Schön renews his demands that she does not attempt to prevent his forthcoming marriage: 'I shall be married within a week; until then keep out of my sight.' Confronted by Lulu's threat of leaving with the Prince for Africa, however, Schön realizes his inability to break his ties with Lulu.

[*SONATA RECAPITULATION: First subject*]
'The man of power weeps', says Lulu triumphantly as Schön's
weakness is finally exposed and he breaks down in tears. 'Now
please leave.'

[*SONATA RECAPITULATION: Transition*]
Lulu fetches writing paper and

[*SONATA RECAPITULATION: Second subject*]
dictates a letter which Schön writes to his fiancée breaking off their
engagement.

ACT II

*SCENE 1. An elegant living room in the German
renaissance style. A flight of steps leads up to a gallery*

[*Recitative*]
Lulu, now married, to Schön, is receiving the Countess Geschwitz,
another of her admirers, who has come to invite her to attend a ball
for women artists.

[*Ballade**]
While Lulu escorts the Countess to the door, Schön bemoans the
fate that has led him to entertain such people in his house: 'The
evening of my life; thirty years' work and this is my family circle.'

[*Cavatina*]
Lulu returns and, despite her pleas that he take the day off, Schön
leaves for the Stock Exchange. The stage is empty for a moment.
Countess Geschwitz surreptitiously enters, crosses the stage and
hides behind a fire screen.

[*Ensemble*]
A trio of Lulu's admirers – an Athlete, a Schoolboy and the old
beggar Schigolch – arrive, as is their custom on the day when Schön
is away at the Stock Exchange. They make themselves comfortable, helping themselves to drinks and cigars. Lulu crosses the stage
and greets them.

[*Canon*]
The three guests sing of their infatuation with Lulu and of their wish (all of them, including Schigolch who makes it clear that he is not, whatever Schön believes, Lulu's father) to marry her.

[*Recitative*]
The Manservant announces the arrival of 'Herr Doktor Schön' – in reality Alwa, although the company take it to mean the return of Lulu's husband. In the confusion that follows, the three admirers try desperately to hide before 'Herr Doktor Schön' appears. The Athlete eventually hides behind the curtains and the Schoolboy under the dining table. Schigolch, wheezing from his asthma, is still slowly making his way up the stairs as Alwa enters.

[*RONDO*]
Alwa's entrance is marked by the first appearance of the lyrical main theme of the Rondo which acts as the formal basis of Act II of the opera. Alwa looks at the retreating figure of Schigolch with astonishment and asks who it is. Lulu explains that he is an old friend who was in the war with Alwa's father.

[*Chorale*]
The music of the Rondo is briefly interrupted as the Manservant enters to set the table and serve hors d'oeuvres.

[*RONDO continued*]
Supposing himself alone with Lulu (the room is, in reality, full of hidden people), Alwa begins to tell her how difficult it has been for him to keep his true feelings for her hidden; as he does so, Dr Schön enters, unnoticed, and overhears the rest of their conversation.

[*Chorale*]
The conversation (and the music of the Rondo) is again interrupted as the Manservant returns to clear the plates.

[*RONDO continued*]
Kissing Lulu's hand, Alwa declares his love for her.

[*Tumultuoso*]
The already absurd situation gradually degenerates into low farce. The Athlete, putting his head out from behind the curtains, sees Dr

Schön, who threatens him with a gun. In an attempt to divert Schön's attention from himself, the Athlete indicates what is going on between Lulu and Alwa and quickly retreats to his hiding place. Schön comes down the stairs and Lulu and Alwa now notice him for the first time. Schön leads Alwa away. In the momentary respite afforded by Schön's absence, the Athlete attempts, unsuccessfully to escape up the stairs before finally hiding behind the door curtain. Schön returns, locks the door and, hoping to reveal the Athlete, pulls the window curtains aside. 'Where has he gone?' asks Schön. 'He's an acrobat', says Lulu calmly.

[*Five-Strophe Aria*]
[*Strophes 1–4*]   Furious, Schön turns on Lulu and castigates her for dragging his name through the mud. The only way out, before Schön becomes so jealous that he kills his own son, is for her to kill herself. He tries to force the revolver into Lulu's hands. She pulls the trigger, firing a shot at the ceiling and in the ensuing panic the Athlete finally makes his escape up the stairs. 'How many more men have you hidden here?' asks Schön as he searches the room and, pulling aside the firescreen, reveals the hidden Countess Geschwitz. He drags the Countess into an adjoining room and locks the door on her. He forces Lulu to take the revolver: 'How can I divorce you when you have become a part of me . . . come, make an end of it.'

[*Lied*]
In one of the two great arias in which she justifies her actions, Lulu reminds Schön that it is not her fault if men have died for her sake. He knew when he married her that she had never pretended to be any other than she is. If he has sacrificed his age to her she has also sacrificed her youth for him.

[*Strophe 5*]   Schön tries to point the revolver at Lulu but is momentarily distracted by a noise from the Schoolboy who is still hiding under the table. As he turns to look in the direction of the noise, Lulu fires five shots and, wounded, Schön collapses. Hearing the shots Alwa rushes down from the gallery and the Schoolboy finally emerges from under the table. Alwa, attempting to lift his father into the bedroom, unlocks the adjoining door and Countess Geschwitz emerges. 'The devil!' gasps Schön as he dies.

[*Arietta*]

Lulu pleads with Alwa not to let her be arrested. He stops her leaving as a banging on the outside door announces the arrival of the police.

INTERLUDE: Film Music

A tumultuous, flickering orchestral interlude accompanies a silent film depicting, in its first half, Lulu's arrest, trial, sentence and imprisonment. The second half of the film depicts the means of her escape from prison: her catching cholera from Countess Geschwitz, her transfer to the isolation hospital and the substitution of the Countess for Lulu. Both the music and the accompanying film have a palindromic structure (the music running backwards from the middle, while the sequence of shots in the second half of the film corresponds to those in the first in reverse order) as a symbol of this crucial turning point in both Lulu's career and in the opera itself. Much of the music of the following scene repeats that of the previous scene in slow motion.

SCENE 2. The same

[*Recitative*]

The curtain rises on the set of the previous scene, now covered with dust sheets and dilapidated after a year's neglect. Alwa, the Countess Geschwitz and the Athlete are awaiting the arrival of Schigolch on whom their plans for Lulu's escape depend.

[*Largo*]

Schigolch arrives and leaves with Geschwitz for the isolation hospital where she will change places with Lulu.[1]

[*Chamber Music II**]

Alone, the Athlete and Alwa are disturbed by a visit from the Schoolboy who, having escaped from the correction centre where his misdemeanours have landed him, has come to tell them of his plan to free Lulu from prison. The Athlete shows him a newspaper story about the murderer of Dr Schön having contracted cholera, and he persuades the Schoolboy that Lulu is dead. The Athlete throws the dejected Schoolboy out of the door as steps are heard from the gallery.

[*Melodrama*]

Weak and leaning heavily on Schigolch's arm, Lulu comes slowly down the stairs. The Athlete is horrified by her appearance (he had planned to make her a partner in his acrobatic act) and leaves, threatening to denounce her to the police. Schigolch also leaves to organize travelling arrangements. Alone with Alwa, Lulu throws off her pretence and, in one of the great moments of the opera, sings a paean to the freedom of which she had been deprived.

[*RONDO*]

The music of the Rondo, constantly interrupted in the previous scene, returns unbroken as, alone at last, Alwa declares his love for Lulu.

[*Hymn*]

They sink together on to the couch, and Alwa sings a passionate hymn in praise of physical love. 'Isn't this the divan on which your father bled to death?' asks Lulu as Alwa buries his head in her lap.

ACT III

SCENE 1. A spacious, white, stuccoed salon

[*Ensemble I*]

The curtain rises on a large group of people in the salon of a casino in Paris. The gaming room with its baccarat table can be seen through the doors at the back of the stage. The Athlete is proposing a toast; there is an animated hubbub of conversation. The company moves into the gaming room, although a few linger behind to ask the Banker about the booming Jungfrau-Railway shares which they have just acquired.

[*Concertante Chorale Variations*]

[*Variations I–II*] Lulu is left alone with the Marquis, who is blackmailing her. The Marquis, a white slave-trader, refuses to accept money from her, but

[*INTERMEZZO 1: The Procurer's Song*]

offers to remain silent if she is willing to accept a job that he has found for her in a Cairo brothel. During this number a solo violin in the orchestra plays, for the first time in the opera, the melody of the Wedekind cabaret song that will form the basis of the subsequent orchestral *Variation* interlude and of the final scene.

[*Intermezzo 2*]
Lulu refuses: 'I know at a hundred paces in the dark if a man is right for me and if I go against this knowledge I feel besmirched.' This, the second number in the opera in which Lulu justifies her actions, is set as a reprise of the first, the *Lied der Lulu* of Act II, scene 1.

[*Variations III–XII*] The Marquis threatens to denounce her to the police as the murderer of Dr Schön. Both the police and the owners of the Egyptian brothel will pay in cash, whereas – apart from the Jungfrau shares with which the Marquis will have nothing to do – Lulu and 'her composer' are penniless. He gives her an hour to decide. 'You can't ask me to sell the only thing that I've ever been able to call my own', says Lulu.

[*Ensemble II*]
The music of the first ensemble returns at a more leisurely pace as the company comes back from the gaming room – everyone, including the bank, has won. In high spirits, they move into the adjoining room where a buffet supper is being served.

[*Duet**]
The Athlete detains Lulu. He has just got engaged and has told his fiancée that he is a wealthy man. He, too, threatens to denounce Lulu to the police unless she can find him money.

[*Pantomime*]
The Athlete joins the others when they return to the gaming room; as they do so the Banker is handed a note telling him of the collapse of the Jungfrau shares.
   Schigolch arrives to ask Lulu for money. In despair Lulu tells him of the Athlete's threats. Together they determine to persuade Countess Geschwitz to lure the Athlete to Schigolch's lodgings. Schigolch will then dispose of the Athlete and push his body out of his window into the river.

[*Cadenza*]
As Lulu and Schigolch move away, the Marquis pushes the Athlete into the salon and warns him not to try to blackmail Lulu. As the

Marquis leaves, the Athlete makes a great show of defiance behind his back.

In an extended musical section that systematically moves backward and forwards between spoken text and cantabile singing, Lulu convinces the Athlete that Countess Geschwitz is infatuated with him and has agreed to lend the money if he is willing to spend the night with her.

The Athlete goes to wait in the buffet room while Lulu persuades Geschwitz that only by spending the night with the Athlete can she help save her life. Horrified by the prospect, the Countess, nonetheless, agrees; she and the Athlete leave for Schigolch's lodgings. Lulu goes quickly into the dining room with the groom with whom she proposes to swap clothes.

[*Ensemble III*]

The music of the earlier ensembles returns at breakneck speed as the doors of the gaming room are thrown open and, in uproar, the company spills into the salon. News of the collapse of the Jungfrau-Railway shares has reached them and they are unsuccessfully trying to persuade the Banker to redeem their now worthless shares. As they drift away, Lulu comes out of the dining room dressed in the groom's clothes and tells Alwa of the impending arrival of the police. They escape as the police commissioner, accompanied by the Marquis, arrives and mistakenly arrests the groom.

INTERLUDE: *VARIATIONS*

The tune heard on the solo violin in the Marquis' *Procurer's Song* (*Intermezzo 1* of the previous scene) now returns as the theme of a set of four variations. The variations of this Interlude return in their entirety during the course of the following scene.

SCENE 2. *An attic room without windows*

[*Scena I**]

The curtain rises (to the sound of Wedekind's tune played by an off-stage wind band in imitation of a barrel-organ) to reveal a miserable attic, lit by a smoking oil lamp. One can hear the sound of the rain on the roof. Schigolch and Alwa await the return of Lulu who is walking the streets on her first night as a prostitute.

They hide as the sound of footsteps announces the arrival of Lulu and her first client.

The music associated earlier with the Medical Specialist (the *Melodrama* and the *Canzonetta* of Act I, scene 1) returns as Lulu and her first client, the Professor, enter. The Professor says nothing throughout the following scene, periodically holding his finger to his lips to show that he wants Lulu also to be silent (the music stops each time he holds up a finger).

[*Scena II**]
Lulu and her client go into an adjoining room and the Medical Specialist's music is replaced by a return of the barrel-organ tune as Alwa and Schigolch search the Professor's pockets – finding only a devotional book *For Pious Pilgrims and those who are devoted to becoming such*.

The sound of the returning Professor, again accompanied by the music of the earlier *Canzonetta*, forces Alwa and Schigolch back into hiding. They re-emerge as he leaves.

More footsteps heard on the stairs ('probably those of a friend coming on his recommendation' says Schigolch) prove to be those of the Countess Geschwitz who arrives bearing Lulu's portrait.

[*Quartet*]
The portrait is nailed to the wall and there develops a rapturous quartet as the four, gazing at the portrait, reflect on what has happened to them. The music of *VARIATION IV* of the earlier orchestral Interlude returns as Lulu, unable to contemplate the picture of what she used to be, returns to the street. Countess Geschwitz follows her.

[*Scena III**]
VARIATION II reappears as Schigolch and Alwa are left alone again. Their conversation is interrupted by the sounds of Lulu returning with her second client. Schigolch returns to his hiding place in the closet, but Alwa refuses and hides beneath his plaid rug. Lulu enters with the Negro. During the following exchange the music associated with the Painter in Act I – the *Monoritmica* and the *Duettino* – returns. Lulu and the Negro argue about money, and Alwa intervenes. The Negro strikes him on the head with a cosh, and he leaves as Alwa collapses dead on the floor.

[*Scene IV**]

Lulu rushes out of the door and the 'funèbre' *VARIATION III* from the orchestral Interlude reappears as Schigolch drags Alwa's body into the cupboard. Schigolch then sets off for the local pub. Alone on stage the Countess contemplates suicide but her reverie is interrupted by the arrival of Lulu with her third client, Jack the Ripper. During the following exchange, as Lulu begs Jack to stay the night and he haggles about payment, the music of the Coda of Dr Schön's Act I Sonata and of the *Cavatina* of Act II returns. Their bargaining is briefly interrupted by a movement from Countess Geschwitz. The music of the Sonata Coda and of Lulu's characteristic Entrance Music make their final appearance as Jack and Lulu go into the adjoining room.

[*Nocturno*]

Over a gently circling, almost static, pattern of notes Countess Geschwitz kneels alone in front of Lulu's portrait and contemplates returning to Germany to study law and fight for women's rights. Her monologue is brutally cut off by Lulu's screams from the adjoining room and by her death-cry as Jack kills her. Geschwitz rushes to Lulu's aid but, as she reaches the door, it is thrown open by Jack who stabs her, too. Jack washes his hands and goes, leaving the Countess once more alone on stage to sing her final *Liebestod* as she dies.

4 *Posthumous history*

To turn to the history of *Lulu* in the fifty years following the composer's death is to plunge into a series of events almost as convoluted and as bizarre as those of the plot of the opera itself.

When Berg died in December 1935 he left behind him a full score of the Prologue and of the whole of Acts I and II of *Lulu*. Of the 1326 bars of Act III Berg had scored some 390 bars: the first 268 bars of scene 1 (that is, almost to the end of the second ensemble) and the two other sections – the *Variation* interlude between scenes 1 and 2, and the finale *Grave* – that appear in the *Symphonic Pieces from 'Lulu'*.

As we have seen, however, Berg began work on the full score only after the short score of the whole opera (including Act III) had been completed in April 1934. The only passages of music not fully notated in the short score of Act III were:

(1) a passage of twenty-four bars in the Quartet of Act III, scene 2, where Berg had written out the main vocal line and the orchestral accompaniment, but had not completed the subsidiary vocal lines (although he had marked the points at which the voices were to enter or stop during the passage);

(2) the passage which opens the final scene of the opera, when the curtain rises to the sound of a *Lautenlied* by Wedekind played by an off-stage barrel-organ. Only the melody, not the accompanying diatonic harmony, is notated in the short score;

(3) a passage of twenty-two bars in the second ensemble of Act III, scene 1, where Berg intended to extend the dialogue between Lulu and the Countess Geschwitz. Although not notated, the short score includes precise directions as to how this extension was to be carried out;

(4) a passage of nineteen bars in the third ensemble of Act III, scene 1, where Berg had written out the main vocal lines but

intended that the subsidiary vocal lines should add a gently mur-
muring background to the foreground conversation. These subsidiary vocal parts were to be realized by doubling fragments of the
existing instrumental accompaniment.

Thus, of the 1326 bars of the final act of *Lulu* only about 87 bars
were not fully notated in Berg's short score and, with one exception, all these 'problematic' passages could be completed in accordance with Berg's own intentions either by following the indications
provided in the score or by doubling the existing instrumental parts.
In the case of the exceptional passage – the barrel-organ music that
opens Act III, scene 2 – the short score itself offers no guidance
about how the melody was to be harmonized. A clear indication of
how Berg intended to complete the passage is, however, to be
found at the end of the *Variation* movement of the *Symphonic
Pieces*, where the first four bars appear fully harmonized and in
Berg's own orchestration. Apart from the filling-in of these 'incomplete' bars, finishing the orchestration and sorting out an intricate
sequence of tempo relationships in the final scene, the score of Act
III was left in a state in which it required only the kind of editorial
attention that is required by any musical score being prepared for
publication.

At the time of Berg's death it was generally agreed by all those
who were in a position to voice an informed opinion that *Lulu* was
not an 'unfinished' work; no one needed to compose any *new* music
(in the way that Süssmayr had to compose original music for the
Mozart *Requiem* or Alfano for Puccini's *Turandot*) in order to
complete Berg's opera. All those who were familiar with the
material were unanimous in their agreement that the score could
and should be completed. Only a few weeks after Berg's death his
publishers wrote to his widow to tell her of Ernst Krenek's opinion
that 'the short score could be completed without great difficulty,
and certainly by a Berg pupil, such as Apostel, whose familiarity
with his working methods could be relied on'.[1] A year later, in his
book on the composer (published in 1937), Berg's pupil and official
biographer, Willi Reich, unequivocally stated that 'The completion
of the instrumentation in a manner consistent with Berg's own style
should be accomplished by a musician familiar with his work.'[2]
Indeed, a prefatory note to the vocal score of Acts I and II, which
Universal Edition published in 1936, stated that the composer 'had
completed the work shortly before his death' and promised that,

although much of Act III remained to be orchestrated, the vocal score of the final act would be published 'in the near future'. By the time this prefatory note appeared, Erwin Stein, who had prepared the vocal score of Acts I and II of *Lulu*, had already completed the vocal score of Act III.

Like Berg's pupils and friends, Helene Berg was also, at this stage, eager to see the work completed. Almost immediately after Berg's death, Erwin Stein, acting on behalf of Berg's widow, approached Schoenberg asking him to complete Act III of *Lulu*. In March 1936 Schoenberg, having studied the surviving material, replied refusing to undertake the work – not because he thought the job impossible, but because he objected to the characterization of the Jewish banker in Act III, scene 1.[3] He, nonetheless, expressed the hope that someone else would finish the score. Helene Berg also approached Webern at about the same time. Webern is reported to have returned the score saying that he did not know what to do after the fourth bar,[4] a statement that is incomprehensible to anyone who has studied Berg's manuscript and can only be explained, as Friedrich Cerha has suggested, by assuming that Webern was frightened by the prospect of working on a music that was stylistically and aesthetically so different from his own.[5] Alfred Schlee of Universal Edition later related how Webern, in March 1946, expressed a wish to 'complete the unfinished parts of Berg's *Lulu*'.[6] According to her own account of the matter, Helene Berg approached Alexander Zemlinsky, too; Zemlinsky's wife has since denied that her husband was ever asked to complete the opera.[7]

The world première of *Lulu* took place at the Stadttheater in Zurich on 2 June 1937 under Robert Denzler. The role of Lulu was sung by Nuri Hazdic, the Countess Geschwitz by Maria Bernhard, Dr Schön by Asger Stig and Alwa by Peter Baxevanos. Amongst the many prominent *émigrés* in the first-night audience was Thomas Mann who wrote in his diary: 'Went to the opera house for the première of Alban Berg's *Lulu* ... *Tout* Zurich. Superlative production of the fragmentary and difficult work. Wedekind's icy and overwrought dialogue is softened by the music which is at its loveliest in the interludes. Often there were *Tristan*-like effects, proving that Wagner was at his most modern and most influential in that work.'[8]

Inevitably the critics were as aware of the political as of the musical significance of the occasion.

It is a sign of the times [wrote the critic of the *Schweizerische Musikzeitung*] that this work can only be given a performance in Zurich. And yet the piece is in no way a danger to the state ... we are left wholly with the impression of a marvellous work, and if the peculiar circumstances of the time overburden our stages, which have still relatively modest means, with the duty of performing such works it is a duty of honour; that our theatre has not refused but has rather produced a magnificent performance is a fact of music-history that will carry its own reward.

Describing the opera as 'the legacy of the great Viennese composer and dramatist' the *Schweizerische Musikzeitung* confidently anticipated the imminent completion of the third act (from 'the existing and detailed sketches'), which would 'complete the curve of the structure' and described the temporary solution that had been adopted for the première:

After the second act had died away the director [Karl] Schmid-Blos came on to the stage, explained the circumstances to the audience and said a few words about the content of Act III. The 'Symphonic Pieces' from Act III, which Berg himself orchestrated, were then played and the closing scene acted, with the scenery indicated.[9]

The anonymous Swiss critic was not to know that the 'temporary' solution adopted by Zürich was to become the standard way of performing *Lulu* for the next forty years.

The Nazi music periodical *Die Musik* was, predictably, less enthusiastic about the work of a composer whose music was officially proscribed in the Third Reich and who was also, moreover, the pupil of a Jewish teacher. Under the heading 'Musical Bolshevism in the Opera', *Die Musik* reprinted a review by Hans Corrodi that had appeared in the *Völkischer Beobachter* of Munich. The review dismissed any apparent success the piece might have had and it explained the dangerous moral and political implications of both *Lulu* and the twelve-note system:

150 years ago Schiller characterized the theatre as being a 'moral institution'. How then is it that the heroines of all the music dramas that have sullied the stages of the world since the beginning of this century have been hysterics, adulterers, courtesans, harlots, prostitutes, perverse monsters, murderesses? ... [This *Lulu*] is a music of prostitutes and pimps, bondsmen and the criminal world. Doubtless very knowing and impressive; a deliberate tearing at the nerves, a brutal whipping of the air, a tortured piling up of anguish, fear and horror ... but these are the old shocks of yesteryear. Berg is a pupil of Schoenberg and, staying true to him, follows him into the realm of twelve-note music, of musical communism: tonality, the basis of music given by nature, which through the natural overtone series and the organization of our ears gives triads, is thrown overboard; all

hierarchies, all priorities, all sense of leadership is put aside in favour of a universal equality; there is no tonic or dominant any more, all twelve notes have equal rights. But since that would result in anarchy and caprice, and therefore the debased instinct of the intellectual shrinks back from it, Schoenberg sought to replace an organic relationship with a new, artificial and arbitrary one. He constructed a system: the twelve notes of the chromatic scale must follow one another always in the same order and none must reappear before all the others have. There is therefore an absolute equality of rights so that, theoretically, all the notes would appear with equal frequency. Berg himself has, by dismantling and rearranging the row, managed, in spite of everything, to preserve some freedom of movement. Moreover, he uses the forms of absolute music ... but it all remains pointless shadow-boxing, for these bloodless schemes and sterile intellectualisms lead a mythical existence that no listener can really perceive. This music is an end not a beginning; it is the expression of the tired, metropolitan intelligence, of European decadence, of the atrophying basis of a world that is becoming extinct. This music is the mirror of that world that staggered into a world war; it comes a quarter of a century too late.

And the success? Hardly even a cool, polite success in front of the otherwise fashion-seeking Zurich public amongst whom there was, for that very purpose, a strong contingent of Jewish internationalists. The time of atonality is past. After 15 years of terror its power has weakened. The child has cried 'The King is without his clothes' and, astonished, the narrow-minded intellectuals and snobs have agreed.[10]

It is perhaps significant that the article that followed this review in *Die Musik* was an anti-semitic piece entitled 'Concerning contemporary Jewish musicians'.

Despite the attempt of *Die Musik* to belittle the Zurich première, it is clear that the production was an enormous success. As a result of this success Helene Berg's attitude to *Lulu* began to change.

She still believed that her duty to Berg necessitated that the *Lulu* material be published and made available, but was now less sure that the scoring should be finished by someone else. The Zurich première had, after all, shown that to perform the opera in a two-act version was an acceptable solution, as she wrote to Hans Heinsheimer, the head of Universal Edition's opera department a few days after the Zurich première:

I can understand the viewpoint of a publishing house which avoids publishing a work that is incomplete and perhaps not capable of being performed or of being a success and therefore represents a risk. But now when the great success of the première must have put aside such justifiable ideas I come back to my wish which you have known for a long time; namely that you publish, as soon as possible, the piano score of Act III, the complete libretto and the score completed up to the point at which the catastrophe struck Alban (Lulu's last sacrifice!) himself.[11]

As Heinsheimer pointed out, however, there was little point in publishing the piano score of Act III unless it was with a view to completing the opera and performing the whole work. 'If we publish the complete Act III in piano score, the press and the theatre directors will also want it to be performed and then we shall again have to face the difficult question of the score's completion.'[12]

The engraving of Erwin Stein's vocal score of Act III was begun in 1937 but was abandoned after seventy pages because of political pressure. Although Austria was at that time still an independent country, and was to remain independent for a few more months before the Anschluss of 12 March 1938 turned it into a province of the German Reich, the artistic life of the country was already largely determined by the policies of the Nazi Cultural Committee. Viennese performances of the music of Berg, Webern and other composers proscribed in Nazi Germany were infrequent and were officially discouraged; the Viennese première of the Berg Violin Concerto took place only because the conductor Otto Klemperer insisted, in the face of opposition from the orchestra and the government officials who all tried to force the cancellation of the concert. In the years after the Anschluss, Universal Edition like other important institutions was 'nazified', its Jewish directors dismissed, and proscribed composers removed from its lists of publications.

The completion of Alban Berg's second (and, given the political climate, unperformable) opera was a matter of no pressing importance.

Among the first important musical events in Vienna after the war were two concert performances of *Lulu* on 15 February and 29 April 1949. Conducted by Herbert Hafner, with Ilona Steingruber singing Lulu, the concerts were organized by Austrian Radio in conjunction with the ISCM. According to the German periodical *Melos* the concerts were preceded by twenty orchestral rehearsals spread over a rehearsal period of eight months. The press was enthusiastic. 'Berg is the Adagio- and espressivo-composer *par excellence* and there are some orchestral interludes in *Lulu* that in their beauty and intensity are only surpassed by *Tristan*', observed *Melos*.[13] 'Berg's handling of the conception in terms of music is wonderful', wrote Desmond Shawe-Taylor in *The New Statesman*[14] who had heard the BBC transmission of the Austrian performance, 'the texture of *Lulu* is softer, more lyrical and still more fascinating in tone-colour than that of *Wozzeck*; frequent use of saxophone and vibraphone lends to parts of the score an insinuating charm and an eerie glitter like nothing else in music.' Both reviews raised the question of the completion of the third act: 'The sooner this act is reconstructed the better, for *Lulu* is yet another instance of the power of music to transfigure the most commonplace or sordid material', wrote Shawe-Taylor. 'The opera is certainly performable in this fragmentary state', observed H. A. Fiechtner in *Melos*, 'yet the composer's widow, who attended the Vienna performance, is contemplating a completion of the final act. A musician from the Schoenberg circle and an Italian composer have been mentioned in this respect.' In fact Friedrich Cerha, the man who would eventually undertake the work of completing the score, was gaining his first experience of the opera by attending almost all the rehearsals for these two Viennese concert performances.

It was with the first post-war stagings of *Lulu* that the completion of Act III became a matter of more than academic interest. The first post-war staged performance of *Lulu* took place in September 1949 at the Teatro del Fenice in Venice as part of the Venice Biennial Festival. Conducted by Nino Sansogno and directed by Giorgio Strehler it attracted little critical attention – so little, in fact, that four years later Mosco Carner, writing of the subsequent Essen production, could describe it as being 'for all I know, the first revival of the opera since its first production in Zürich in 1937'.[15]

It was as a result of the 1953 Essen production that the necessity of completing Act III began to be more widely discussed. As Carner said in his *Time and Tide* review:

The reason for this neglect must, I assume, lie in the fact that the final scenes of the third act are incomplete and, needless to say, staging unfinished opera is a much more tricky problem than performing unfinished symphonies. In the production of the Essen company, the text of these scenes was spoken to the music Berg orchestrated for inclusion in the so-called *Lulu-Symphony* consisting of the five excerpts which we sometimes hear in the concert hall. If the opera is to be seen on the stage this is at present the only solution. But ... the sketches were left in an advanced enough state — musically they are in fact complete – for someone with the necessary feeling for Berg's orchestral style to translate them into full score and thus rescue from a shadow-existence his last opera which as a piece of musico-dramatic writing is the equal of *Wozzeck*.

Four years later there appeared the first German version of Hans Redlich's book on Berg, in which he spoke strongly in favour of the opera being completed. The same year also saw the staging of a new and much acclaimed *Lulu* by the Hamburg Opera with Helga Pilarczyk as Lulu and Toni Blankenheim as Dr Schön.

By 1960, Frau Helene Berg had imposed a complete ban on Act III; not only was the third act to remain incomplete and unpublished, but nothing was to be written about it and no one was to be allowed access to the material.

There began a gradual process of what can only be called 'disinformation', the publication of deliberately misleading or doubtful information, the main purpose of which was to cast doubts on the possibility of finishing the work, to foster the belief that the score was little more than a fragment, and to discourage scholars and, more importantly, opera companies from enquiring about the piece. The vocal score of Acts I and II was republished with the original prefatory note replaced by one that read: 'The opera is to be performed as a fragment. Only the first two acts were fully orchestrated by Berg. Of Act III only those portions which Berg included in the *Lulu* suite – the Variations and the final Adagio – are scored.' Not only had the original note's announced intention of publishing a vocal score of Act III disappeared, but the original reference to the fact that Berg had completed a short score of the final act and the admission that not 'only those portions included in the *Lulu Suite*' had been orchestrated were completely omitted. When in 1963 Willi Reich published a reworked and partly rewritten version of his book on Berg, the sentence urging the completion of *Lulu* by someone 'familiar with Berg's style' had simply disappeared. Despite the pleas of such distinguished figures as Igor Stravinsky, Theodor Adorno and Hans Redlich, and a series of scholarly articles by the eminent American composer and Berg scholar George Perle refuting the arguments in favour of non-publication (one of which is reproduced in the documentary section of the present book) Helene Berg refused to reverse her decision. In the will which she made in 1969 and which was published after her death on 30 August 1976, Helene Berg repeated her demand that 'No one be allowed to examine the manuscript of Act III of *Lulu* nor is anyone to be allowed to study the photocopy in the possession of Universal Edition.'[16]

For the first forty years of its stage life *Lulu* was, thus, condemned to be performed as an incomplete two-act torso, a handicap which few operas could survive and which, in the case of *Lulu*, had a devastating effect on both the finely calculated musical architecture and on the meaning of the opera. It says much for the vitality and dramatic power of Berg's music that, even in this form, *Lulu* established itself as part of the operatic repertoire and attracted to it a number of notable interpreters such as Evelyn Lear, Helga Pilarczyk, Anneliese Rothenberger and Anja Silja.

The first Viennese staged performance of *Lulu* took place under Karl Böhm at the Theater an der Wien on 9 June 1962 as part of the Vienna Festival. Evelyn Lear played Lulu, Paul Schöffler sang Dr Schön, Gisela Litz sang Countess Geschwitz and Rudolf Schock was Alwa. In a review in *Melos* headed '*Lulu*: Highpoint of the Vienna Festival' Lothar Knessl observed: 'The closing scene will remain problematic as long as no one takes it upon himself to orchestrate, and thus make performable, the material of Act III which Berg left almost unbroken in piano and short score.'[17] Knessl was not to know that the day after the Theater an der Wien première the young composer Friedrich Cerha had gone to Universal Edition to ask to see the score and short score of Act III of *Lulu*. 'Before that performance', said Cerha, 'I was mainly interested in the musical language and sonorities of the work, now it was above all the structural and formal aspects that interested me, the complex system of relationships that grows in scope throughout the work and makes it a closed, living organism.'[18] From 1962 onwards Friedrich Cerha, with the knowledge and encouragement of Universal Edition, worked on a realization of Act III of *Lulu*.

The most important of the work to be done has been described above. In order to complete the task Cerha had available to him: (a) Berg's short score, sketches and serial charts for the act; (b) Berg's orchestration of the first 268 bars of Act III scene 1 and the last two movements of the *Symphonic Pieces*; (c) a vocal score by Berg of the last 17 bars of the opera; (d) Erwin Stein's vocal score of the whole act and (e) Berg's libretto. Amongst the sketches for *Lulu* was also Berg's typed copy of the dramatis personae (corresponding to that suggested, on the basis of internal musical evidence, by George Perle) which enabled Cerha to correct the obvious errors in the dramatis personae in the previously published score of the opera. Other sketches and manuscripts – including the missing text of the Quartet in Act III, scene 2 and the final draft of the scenario for the 'Film Music' Interlude of Act II – have been discovered since Cerha completed his work; the results of these discoveries have been integrated into the new two-volume miniature score of the opera and into more recent editions of the vocal score of Act III.

Despite a court action by the Alban Berg Foundation (a foundation set up by Helene Berg to manage the Berg estate after her death) which attempted to gain an injunction stopping the performance, the complete three-act *Lulu* received its world première at the Paris Opera on 24 February 1979 under Pierre Boulez. The director was Patrice Chereau and the designer Richard Peduzzi. Lulu was sung by Teresa Stratas, the Countess Geschwitz by Yvonne Minton, Dr Schön by Franz Mazura, Alwa by Kenneth Riegel and Schigolch by Toni Blankenheim.

On 28 July of the same year, the three-act *Lulu* had its first American performance (and the first performance of the work in Arthur Jacobs' English translation) at the Santa Fe Opera House in a performance conducted by Michael Tilson Thomas and directed by Colin Graham. Nancy Shade sang Lulu. The winter season of 1979/80 saw three other productions of the complete *Lulu*: in Zurich in September in a production by Götz Friedrich conducted by Ferdinand Leitner, in Frankfurt in October in a production by Harry Kupfer conducted by Michael Gielen and in Berlin in January 1980 in a Joachim Herz production conducted by Joachim Willert at the Komische Oper. The season also saw the emergence of three new Lulus in Carole Farley (Zurich), Slavka Taskova-Paoletin (Frankfurt) and Ursula Reinhardt-Kiss (Berlin).

It was with the 1980/1 season, however, that the three-act *Lulu* finally came into its own, with six major opera companies including the work in their repertoire. Indeed, the opening of the season in October 1980 saw three new productions open within a few days of one another: on 2 October in Amsterdam (in a production by the Netherlands Opera Company, directed by Rhoda Levine and conducted by Hans Vonk, and with a cast that included Teresa Stratas as Lulu); on 14 October in Toronto (in a production by Lotfi Mansouri conducted by Kenneth Montgomery with Claudia Cummings as Lulu) and on 19 October in Bonn (in a production by Uwe Kreyssig, conducted by Jan Krenz with Ursula Reinhardt-Kiss as Lulu). In December 1980 *Lulu* opened the season at the Metropolitan Opera House in New York, and two more productions opened during the season, one at the Teatro San Carlo in Lisbon on 4 February and one at Covent Garden, London on 6 February 1981.

Lulu had its Austrian première in the Landestheater in Graz on

17 October 1982 (when, for the first time, Friedrich Cerha conducted his own realization of Act III), and a year later the complete three-act opera finally reached Vienna when a production at the State Opera conducted by Lorin Maazel, directed by Wolfgang Weber and with sets by Allen Charles Klein opened on 24 October 1983.

We need not, now that the complete *Lulu* has been played throughout Europe and America and has firmly established itself within the repertoire, give details of the thirty or so productions of the opera that have taken place since its première in Paris a decade ago. Some productions are worthy of mention, however, simply because they throw into sharp focus a problem that began with the Paris première and that has plagued the three-act *Lulu* ever since.

The première of the complete *Lulu* in February 1979 generated what, for a twentieth-century opera, must have been an unprecedented amount of interest.[19] Throughout Europe performances were broadcast and televised, radio programmes were devoted to discussions of the work and the background to the opera was described in detail by the press. Nor was this interest confined to the specialist periodicals, music programmes, the arts pages of 'quality' newspapers or those other sections of the media that one might expect to concern themselves with so important an artistic event.

It would be naïve to assume that the enormous amount of publicity that preceded the première sprang entirely from an interest in Berg's music. The *risqué* subject of the opera and its tortuous posthumous history – the composer's premature death, the intervention of the Nazis, the widow's refusal to allow anyone to complete, or even see, the score of the third act and, finally, a scholarly dispute that had, in one way or another, involved many of the most respected composers and scholars of our time – were, in themselves, enough to make a good story. The publication, some eighteen months earlier, of George Perle's articles on 'The Secret Programme of the *Lyric Suite*', articles which first revealed the extent to which one of Berg's most frequently performed works embodied arcane references to his involvement with a woman other than his wife, had, however, generated a much more general interest in the *Lulu* première. To some Perle's revelations suggested the possibility that Helene Berg's embargo on Act III of the opera might, in some way, have been linked to her knowledge of her husband's extra-marital liaisons (that she might perhaps have associated the figure of Lulu with that of the other woman in Berg's life) and gave the whole *Lulu* affair a whiff of scandal that inevitably attracted the attention of the popular press.

The first night was attended by a galaxy of notable figures from the worlds of politics and the arts: 'Everybody was there . . .', observed *The Guardian*, 'Helmut Schmidt was there and so was Raymond Barre and, a couple of seats away from Wieland Wagner, even Mr Heath.'[20] The première was universally acknowledged to be an event of historic significance. It was, said *The Observer*, a 'red-letter day in the annals of opera'[21], while *The Guardian* described it as 'the musical event of the decade, if not of the post-war years'. 'Rarely since the days of Meyerbeer or the Paris version of *Don Carlos* can this ancient institution have been so signally the centre of the operatic world', commented *The Financial Times*.[22] Yet, while recognizing the importance of the event, the critics were unanimous in their condemnation of the production which the work received at the Paris Opera. Patrice Chereau's staging, said *The Observer*, was 'the real weakness of the evening' and, according to *The Financial Times*, created more problems than it solved. It was, thought *The Guardian*, 'a wilful . . . perverse . . . and finally defective production', a production which, *The Sunday Telegraph* observed, 'perversely contradicted the stage directions of the libretto'.[23] Writing in *Opera*, Arthur Jacobs (who, having produced an English translation of the libretto for Universal Edition, was thoroughly familiar with the work) questioned how Pierre Boulez could have 'tolerated (indeed presumably nominated) a producer prepared to distort the composer's essence':

Mr Chereau has gone further in deliberately (because one cannot suppose it was by carelessness) perverting the whole operatic method of Berg in *Lulu*. This score enshrines perhaps the closest correspondence between music, character, movement and gesture ever imagined. In the second act, when Lulu compels Dr Schön to write the renunciation of his bride, the singer of Schön's part finds in his part the notes he is supposed to be *thinking* as he writes down the words to Lulu's dictation. No character is introduced in any scene who does not have musical cues. Chereau on the contrary brings in 'extras' – servants, party guests, theatrical people – who have no cues and thus in the deepest sense no presence . . . they are not merely superfluous, they negate.[24]

Jacobs' perceptive review neatly pinpoints what has been a constantly recurring problem of productions of *Lulu*. There is perhaps no opera in the entire operatic repertoire in which the composer has been more precise in his demands about staging than was Berg in *Lulu*. Throughout Berg's score the entrances and exits, sometimes even the individual movements, of the different characters are indicated in the greatest detail. In Act II, scene 1, for example, the points at which the Manservant enters, at which the Schoolboy and the Acrobat move, and at which Countess Geschwitz appears and disappears are all clearly marked in the score; and each of these movements on stage is accompanied by a fragment of the music associated with the character concerned. Throughout the whole opera there is no entrance or exit which is not musically indicated in this way. To insist that a producer respect Berg's demands about the way in which a scene is staged is not pedantic. Berg's directions are not impractical 'academic' demands of a kind that can be ignored by those who regard themselves as 'practical men of the theatre'. As Andrew Porter wrote in his review of the Metropolitan Opera's production of the complete *Lulu*: 'Actions are 'notated' almost like a musical line: arrows indicate exactly where they should occur ... displacing the moves or inventing different actions has an effect comparable to displacing Berg's instrumental entries by a few bars or writing new musical lines.'[25] Even the tiniest details of the action are mapped into the intricate musical structure of the work – details such as, for example, the point at the beginning of Act II when, as George Perle has shown, Lulu's gesture of acknowledgment of Countess Geschwitz's gift of flowers coincides precisely with the appearance of the one note that can only derive from the Countess's set.[26] Berg himself has stage-directed the piece; and the musical structure and dramatic effect of Berg's score depend on the observations of his stage directions.

Productions which treated Berg's requirements cavalierly were not uncommon in the years during which *Lulu* was still performed as a two-act torso, when it was at least possible to argue that such directorial liberties could be excused on the grounds that the absence of Act III obscured the overall plan and dramatic method of the work. Yet since, and perhaps as a result of, the Paris production of the complete three-act *Lulu* the work has been subjected to a number of productions that display a shocking ignorance of the most elementary principles of Berg's musico-dramatic organization. The 1981 production by Götz Friedrich at Covent Garden was typical of many recent *Lulu* productions.

Here, in Friedrich's production, Berg's careful and precisely notated correlation of music and stage action was totally destroyed. 'Sometimes I feel that there's almost no connection between what's happening on the stage and what I'm doing in the pit', remarked the conductor Sir Colin Davis in an interview which appeared in *The Times* on the morning of the Covent Garden première; in the event it proved to be a comment that had a significance other than that intended. In Friedrich's production Berg's stage direction counted for nothing; Berg's characters appeared before or after their musical cues and wandered freely around the stage when they should have been invisible to the audience. Similarly, Friedrich (like Chereau before him) introduced a host of figures – dancers, workers, attendants to the Prince – who have no place in the opera and thus, unlike every figure in Berg's score, have no musical identity.

An example of Friedrich's misunderstanding of Berg's musico-dramatic method was the handling of that moment towards the beginning of Act II, scene 1 when, Dr Schön having left for the Stock Exchange, the stage is empty;

Countess Geschwitz, who has left the stage some time before, re-enters, crosses the stage and hides behind the firescreen where she remains unseen until much later in the scene when Schön pulls the firescreen aside to reveal her whereabouts. The moment at which Geschwitz re-enters is clearly indicated in the score by six bars of the music associated with the figure of the Countess, which accompany her movement across the stage. As the Countess disappears behind the firescreen, her characteristic music disappears and is not heard again until she reappears from behind the firescreen later in the scene. In Friedrich's chaotic production of this scene, however, the Countess was unremittingly active – appearing in the background during the number which precedes Schön's leaving for the Stock Exchange and prowling around ceaselessly during that section of the scene when she is supposed to be hidden from view. Indeed, almost the only time when the Countess was not on the move during Friedrich's production of this scene was during those bars when Berg specifically requires her to cross the stage. The music of the six bars which should accompany her crossing of the stage thus lost its *raison d'être* and was reduced to a meaningless accompaniment to an action performed by another character.[27]

Faced with such basic mistakes it hardly seemed worth mentioning those more detailed aspects of the production to which one might otherwise have taken exception; such details as Schigolch's constant asthmatic wheezing (when the points at which he is supposed to gasp for breath are clearly indicated in the score and are always

accompanied by a characteristic 'asthma rhythm') were minor
irritants.

Apologists for such productions (usually members of the production team itself) frequently argue that the liberties taken give –
in some way that is never explained – greater insight into the 'true'
meaning of *Lulu* than could be obtained by simply following Berg's
own direction (an insight denied not only to those of us outside the
production team but also to Berg himself). It is an argument that
was first voiced by Boulez at the time of the Paris première, when a
heated public discussion at IRCAM produced from the audience
(and especially from the writer and broadcaster Dominique
Jameux) a number of comments highly critical of Chereau's production. Defending the production Boulez remarked:

> What a load of codswallop it all is, in fact – this obsession with the time and
> place of the action and this minute following of stage directions. What
> contempt it shows for the real meaning of the work. What a pharisaical
> literal-mindedness! What a failure to understand the autonomous exist-
> ence of the work itself in relation to its creators . . . What exactly are the
> complaints against Chereau? . . . That he replaced Wedekind's attic by a
> basement public lavatory? That he changed the date from 1900 to 1930?
> That he made the Medizinalrat two different characters? . . . bringing in
> the crowd unnecessarily? As if the real structure and significance were not
> more clearly revealed by a single one of Chereau's modifications than by
> any slavish following of Berg's stage directions.[28]

Boulez did not, could not explain how a 'single one of Chereau's
modifications' revealed 'the real structure and significance' of the
piece more than following Berg's directions would have done.

Such a defence can, of course, be used to exonerate any
production and to excuse any indulgence or liberty. In February
1988 the Théâtre de la Monnaie in Brussels mounted what was
perhaps the most bizarre and absurd production of *Lulu* yet staged;
a production by Ruth Berghaus that was both stunningly simple-
minded and literal, in the way that it interpreted some things that
are suggested or lightly touched on in Berg's opera, and at the same
time overwhelmingly arrogant in its complete disregard of Berg's
detailed stage directions and, indeed, of much of the plot.

> Anyone who wants to get to know Berg's *Lulu*, [said *The Guardian*'s critic
> Gerald Larner] should read the libretto, study the score, buy the Boulez
> recording but have nothing to do with the production at La Monnaie in
> Brussels until they are certain of the facts. East Berlin's most formidable
> producer is sublimely indifferent to the facts if they happen to obstruct her
> purpose . . . the Painter does not paint, the portrait of Lulu, which follows

her through every stage in her degradation, does not exist; in its place there is a vaguely figural transparent plastic sculpture . . .[29]

This 'plastic sculpture' acted as a screen on to which, as Wolf Dietrich Peter noted in his review in *Fonoforum*, were projected lights and images to symbolize the fantasies which the men in the opera projected on to Lulu herself. It was a *Lulu* that was not only anti-realistic and, as the *Frankfurter Allgemeine Zeitung* observed, 'didactic and dangerously over-symbolic',[30] but it also deliberately misrepresented some aspects of the opera. 'Not content with the film sequence which Berg calls for in Act Two', wrote Andrew Clark in *The Financial Times*, 'Berghaus daubs the whole perform-ance with surrealist projections.'[31] One such projection showed Lulu and Geschwitz, having consummated their love, careering down a road in bed together. At no point in Berg's opera is there any suggestion that Geschwitz's love for Lulu is consummated. At a public discussion of the production, the Berghaus production team, like that of the team of the earlier Paris première, argued that their approach had been faithful to Berg's intentions and had given the audience an insight into the 'real meaning' of the opera.

In the earlier *Wozzeck* volume in this series I suggested that 'from the earliest beginnings of the form, in the last years of the sixteenth century, the problem of opera has been that of reconciling . . . the demands of the music with those of the dramatic action'.[32] It seems paradoxical, therefore, that *Lulu*, which solves this musico-dramatic problem as perfectly as any work in the whole of musical literature, should have fared so badly at the hands of opera directors. One reason for this may simply be that, as a result of Berg's premature death and the subsequent fifty-year delay in staging the complete work, *Lulu* is still an opera without a performance history; there is, in the case of *Lulu*, no collection of writings by Berg himself on the opera (as there is dealing with the interpretation of *Wozzeck*) and no contemporary performance tradition on which a director can draw.

Another possible, and more suggestive, reason for the unfortu-nate stage history of the three-act *Lulu* may have something to do with the nature of the work itself. In 1987 Scottish Opera staged a fine production of the complete *Lulu* directed by John Cox and conducted by John Mauceri; it was a production that followed Berg's directions in every important respect and was, in the opinion of the present writer, one of the best productions of the work yet staged. The British critics, who had acclaimed Friedrich's production at the Royal Opera House, gave the Scottish production a very cool reception, complaining that Beverly Morgan's Lulu was not 'devastatingly sexy' (*The Guardian*),[33] 'not nasty enough by half' and gave 'no sense of predetermined manipulation' (*Music and Musicians*),[34] lacked 'sheer animalism' (*Northern Echo*)[35] and did not project a 'seductive threat and cynical bestiality although she moves prettily and looks good' (*The Independent*).[36] Finding Miss Morgan's Lulu 'neither predator nor prey' the critic of *The Financial Times* went as far as to say that he (significantly, all the critics quoted above were men) found her a 'tiresome character' who 'one almost feels deserves no better than she gets in the end'.[37] There could perhaps be no more telling, and no more ironic, illustration of the subject at the heart of *Lulu* than the similarities between the way in which the characters in the piece project their fantasies on to Lulu and that in which directors and critics of the production project their own sexual fantasies, obsessions and fears on to the opera itself.

5 The formal design

In the letter to Schoenberg of 7 August 1930 quoted in chapter 2 Berg complained that the progress of his work on *Lulu* was being slowed down not only because the need 'to cut four-fifths of the Wedekind original' made 'the selection of the remaining fifth torture', but also because of the difficulty of 'making the text fit the musical forms (large and small) without destroying Wedekind's idiosyncratic language'.[1] 'Making the text fit the musical form' was, to Berg, a vital step in producing a work that met his conception of music drama as a genre in which the musical and dramatic design were inextricably linked; a genre in which the musical structure fulfilled all the requirements of self-contained instrumental music while, at the same time, reflecting both the overall shape and the most detailed nuances of the drama. Such an intimate relationship between the demands of 'absolute' musical structure and those of dramatic action could only be achieved by the composer acting as his own librettist.

In *Wozzeck* the large-scale formal plan of the opera seems to have emerged only during the course of Berg's work on the piece; in *Lulu*, as chapter 2 has shown, he had a clear idea of the large-scale formal design almost from the outset. At a very early stage in his work on *Lulu*, Berg realized that the dramatic shape of the two Wedekind plays suggested a symmetrical arch-shaped musical structure, a structure centred on the point at the end of the first play when, having murdered Schön, Lulu's ascent of the ladder of bourgeois society documented in *Earth Spirit* becomes a gradual descent into the nightmare world of the final scene of *Pandora's Box*. Since Berg had an almost obsessional fondness for such symmetrical structures, the possibility of imposing such a shape may well have been one of the things that attracted him to the *Lulu* plays at the outset. Within the three acts, the crux of the opera is the Film Music at the very heart of the piece – the palindromic orchestral interlude at the centre of the central act which stands as a symbol of this turning point of both Lulu's career and the opera as a whole. The importance of the Film Music as the focal point of the symmetrical dramatic structure is further emphasized by the fact that the two scenes that surround it (Act II, scenes 1 and 2) are the only scenes in the opera which have the same set, and by the fact that much of the music of the second scene repeats that of the first in (according to Berg's own indication) 'slow motion'.

The key to the intricate musical structure of *Lulu* (and, as I shall argue in chapter 8, to the meaning of the opera) lies in Berg's decision to double the roles of Lulu's three husbands in the first half of the opera with those of her three clients in the final scene of Act III. Originally, as the letter to Schoenberg quoted earlier reveals, Berg had thought of underlining the quasi-palindromic dramatic structure of the work by having the singers of the earlier roles themselves return in *reverse* order – that is, by doubling the role of Dr Schön with that of the first client, the Painter with the second client and the Medical Specialist with Jack the Ripper. It is not clear at what point Berg abandoned this idea and adopted the more effective (and more practical) arrangement of having the role of Jack doubled with that of Dr Schön.

The reappearance of these doubles in Act III, scene 2 initiates a series of recapitulations in which large sections of music from earlier in the opera acquire a new emotional and dramatic meaning. Thus, the music of the *Monoritmica* of Act I, scene 2 (the music which originally led up to the death of the Painter) reappears in Act III when Lulu's second client, the Negro – a role played by the same performer as played the Painter earlier in the opera – kills Alwa.

Similarly, but more disturbing in its effect, the music of the Sonata Coda returns in Act III, scene 2 as Jack (played by the performer who also takes the role of Dr Schön) haggles with Lulu about money immediately before he murders her. Not only do the earlier associations of the Coda with Schön's inability to free himself of Lulu (symbolized by the repetitions of the opera's 'fate rhythm' embodied in the Coda theme) now acquire a new ironic significance, but the contrast between the intensity of the music and the horror of the events depicted on stage sets up an emotional ambiguity that affects the listener's view of everything that has happened earlier in the work. I shall discuss the emotional and dramatic significance of these musical recapitulations in greater detail in chapters 7 and 8.

The use of the same performer in more than one role is not confined to the doubling of Lulu's husbands and clients, although these doublings have the most important musical and dramatic significance. The Prince in Act I, scene 3, the Manservant in Act II, scene 1 and the Marquis in Act III, scene 1 are also played by a single performer and share the same musical material, an arrangement which, according to the comments in Berg's sketches, is meant to draw attention to the three different aspects of slavery (through marriage, servitude and the brothel, respectively) which these three roles embody.[2] The other triple role in the opera (that of the Wardrobe Mistress, the Schoolboy and the Groom) has no dramatic significance, and the three characters are not related musically.[3]

These repetitions – not only of short passages, as in *Wozzeck*, but also of extensive blocks of music – are one of the bases of the formal and dramatic structure of the opera. In some cases the repetitions underline structural symmetries: the shared material between the two scenes of Act II, for example, or the reprise of much of the music of the scene between Lulu and Schigolch in Act I, scene 2 in the similar scene between the same two characters in Act III, scene 1. In other cases the repetitions draw our attention to the pyschological and dramatic similarities between different events and situations. The repetition of a large part of the *Lied der Lulu* from Act II, scene 1 in the *Concertante Chorale Variations* of Act III, scene 1, for example, links the only two numbers in the opera in which Lulu offers a justification for her actions. Similarly the reappearance of the music of the *Duettino* between Lulu and the Painter in Act I, scene 2 as the music to the *Cavatina* of Act II, scene 1 (when Lulu asks Schön to spend the day with her) points to the fact that Schön, like the Painter, is beginning to take Lulu for granted.

At the same time, *Lulu* is a 'number' opera, using the vocal forms traditionally associated with opera – Recitative, Aria, Duet, Arioso, Quartet and so on. Although the division into different numbers is less aurally distinct in *Lulu* than it is in works such as *Oedipus Rex, The Rake's Progress* or the 'new opera' of Weill's *Mahagonny* and *Die Bürgschaft*, the beginnings and ends of these separate formal units are clearly articulated, and the different numbers are clearly indicated in the score. As I shall show in chapter 8, the decision to use such traditional operatic forms springs from, and has a direct bearing on, one of the central topics of the opera.

Interpenetrating this sequence of vocal numbers are three larger musical structures (one in each act of the opera) based on the 'absolute' forms of abstract instrumental music. Each of the three acts of the opera is thus dominated by one of these large-scale 'abstract' forms, a form which embodies the main dramatic idea of the act and the constituent parts of which appear at dramatically appropriate points.

A consideration of the handling of the Sonata movement which dominates Act I will demonstrate the way in which these large forms function. The Sonata Allegro movement of Act I is associated with Dr Schön's attempts to end his relationship with Lulu and to marry a 'respectable young lady'. The Sonata exposition and the first reprise appear in Act I, scene 2 (as in the Sonata structure of Act II, scene 1 of *Wozzeck*, Berg's exposition is immediately followed by a 'written-out' – or, more accurately, rewritten – repeat); the development and recapitulation in Act I, scene 3.

The thematic structure of the exposition follows that of the standard symphonic first movement but (again, as in *Wozzeck*) the libretto is arranged in such a way that each section of the exposition is associated with a specific verbal idea – in the words of Berg's letter to Schoenberg the text 'has been made to fit' the musical form. The following diagram outlines the relationship between the thematic and textual structure of the exposition:

EXPOSITION b. 533–624

First subject b. 533–53:

The Sonata exposition of Act I, scene 2 begins as Schön first turns his attention to the reason for his visit. The First subject represents Schön's public persona as a figure of power, prestige and influence. He demands that Lulu stop seeking him ('I've been saying for two years that you must stop coming to see me. If Walter weren't such a child he would have been on to your escapades long ago').

The First subject theme (Ex. 1) is the most important of the themes associated with Dr Schön throughout the opera:

Ex. 1

1/2 b.533

Allegro energico
marc.

f Str.

Bridge passage b. 554–86

The Bridge passage, which in Berg's own formal sketch is simply headed 'The men', is associated with Schön's attempts to rid himself of Lulu by arranging to have her married.

Section (a) b. 554–61

(Lulu: He sees nothing; neither me nor himself. He is blind. He calls me 'treasure' and 'little bird'. What am I to him? I'm nothing but his woman.)

Section (b) b. 561–78

(Schön: I've married you off twice. You live in luxury, I've created a position for him. If that's not enough for you and he doesn't notice – leave me out of it!)

Section (c) b. 579–86

> The music and text of Sections (a) and (b) above together are then combined as shown in the following example:

Ex. 2

Second subject b. 587–614

The second subject group is associated with Schön's fiancée and his wish to marry a respectable young lady ('I've become engaged; I want to give my bride a respectable house'). The decision to set this part of the text as a Gavotte and Musette is meant to symbolize Schön's desire for respectability, the 'old-fashioned' baroque forms representing here (as they do in the opening scene of *Wozzeck*) bourgeois conventionality of outlook.

Ex. 3

I/2 b.586

Coda b. 615–24

Schön's love for Lulu and his inability to break free
The theme of the Sonata Coda is the most important in the opera, representing not only the love between Schön and Lulu, but also Schön's (literally) fatal ability to free himself from the ties of this love. Its significance will be discussed in detail later.

Ex. 4

I/2 b.615

FIRST REPRISE b. 625–68/958–92

The textual plan of the first reprise follows that of the exposition, the same or related topics of conversation appearing to the same music as before:

First subject b. 625–32

Schön: Leave me out of it. If you owe me anything don't stand in my way.

Bridge b. 633–40

Schön: I had hoped that married to a healthy young man you would at least have been satisfied.

Second subject b. 641–65

Lulu: What could I have against your marriage? But you deceive yourself if you think that your getting married means that you can at last express your contempt for me.

Coda b. 664–8

After two bars the reprise of the Coda (Schön: 'I must at last have my hands free') is interrupted by the appearance of the Painter who has been disturbed by the sounds of their quarrelling. At this point the reprise of the Coda is interrupted by a new, self-sufficient section, the *Monoritmica* (b. 669-957) during which Schön tells the Painter of Lulu's past and demands that he supervise his wife more carefully. The Painter, shocked by Schön's revelations, kills himself, and the police are summoned. As the police arrive the curtain falls and – after an interruption of almost 300 bars – the orchestra reverts to the reprise of the Coda b. 958–92 which now becomes the orchestral interlude in Act I, between scenes 2 and 3.

The development and the recapitulation of the Sonata movement appear in Act I, scene 3. Having fainted on stage at the sight of Schön and his fiancée in the cabaret audience, Lulu returns to her dressing room to be confronted once again by Schön, who renews the argument from the previous scene.

DEVELOPMENT b. 1209–88

With the associations between particular musical and verbal ideas already established in the exposition and the first reprise, the musical course of the Sonata development is determined by the verbal course of the argument between Schön and Lulu. Here and in the final recapitulation, as in much of *Lulu*, Berg uses these established musical–textual relationships as a means of commenting, in the most subtle and telling ways, on the dramatic action. Thus, for example, when Lulu tells the horrified Schön of the Prince's proposal to take her to Africa, her words are accompanied by the theme of the Bridge passage. Through its return at this point, the theme, which was originally associated with Schön's supposed wish to rid himself of Lulu by marrying her off, now acts as an ironic comment on Schön's essential weakness and his capacity for self-deception.

RECAPITULATION b. 1289–1361

First subject b. 1289–98

The First subject, which was originally associated with Schön's demands that he and Lulu stop meeting, returns at the point at which Schön breaks down and admits defeat. 'He weeps', sings Lulu triumphantly, 'the man of authority weeps.'

Bridge passage b. 1299–1303

The Bridge is reduced to a few, predominantly instrumental, bars that accompany Lulu's handing writing-paper to Schön.

Second subject b. 1304–55

The enormously extended Second subject group, which was originally associated with Schön's hopes of marrying a 'respectable young lady', now, with bitter irony, returns as the 'Letter Duet', the music to which Lulu dictates to Schön the note that he will send to his fiancée breaking off their engagement.

Coda b. 1356–61

The Sonata movement, and the act, end with the Coda theme, which has already appeared briefly in the instrumental parts of the previous section, accompanying the words 'I write this at the side of the woman who rules me' at b. 1336–41. The Coda theme now makes its first appearance in the opera as a vocal phrase as Schön, foreseeing the fateful consequence of what he has just done, sings the prophetic words 'Now comes the execution'.

The relation between musical and textual ideas in the Rondo which dominates Act II is less specific, and the musico-dramatic structure of the whole correspondingly less intricate, than that of the Sonata. The Rondo is associated with Alwa's declarations of love for Lulu. In Act II, scene 1, the love scene between Alwa and Lulu is constantly interrupted by the various admirers hidden around the room, by the appearance of the Manservant who is serving a meal and, eventually, by the interjections of Dr Schön who, returning unnoticed, overhears the conversation. The musical structure of the first statement of the Rondo is correspondingly fragmented, its constituent parts separated by music associated with the other characters in the scene. The main Rondo theme (see Ex. 5) is the most important of the thematic ideas associated with Alwa throughout the opera.

Ex. 5
II/i b.243

poco f espress.

The following diagram summarizes the musical and dramatic plan of the scene; the main sections of the Rondo are indicated on the left of the diagram and interventions on the right.

RONDO		INTERRUPTIONS
b. 243–9 *Principal theme*		
	... b. 250–61	The Manservant sets the table
b. 262–7 *Bridge*		
b. 268–73 *Subordinate theme*		
	... b. 274	Dr Schön enters and overhears
b. 275–80 *Subordinate theme (contd.)*		
b. 281–6 *Principal theme*		
	... b. 287–97	Manservant re-enters. Dr Schön comments
b. 298–306 *Principal theme*		
b. 306–9 *Transition*		
	... b. 310–17	Athlete looks out and hides again
b. 318–28 *Concluding theme*		
b. 329–36 *Codetta*		

The second love-scene in the opera appears at the end of Act II, scene 2 when, Schigolch having left to arrange their escape from Germany, Lulu and Alwa are left alone. The interpolated passages which interrupted the earlier love duet (the sections on the right of the diagram) are now excised and the whole Rondo runs without a break, beginning (b. 1001–05) with a middle section devoted to the subordinate theme and continuing with a recapitulation in which the subordinate theme and the transition are omitted.

Ex. 6

Act III is dominated by a set of Variations on a theme by Wedekind (see Ex. 6). Originally the tune of a song about prostitution, the melody here becomes a symbol of Lulu's descent to the life of a street walker. The Wedekind theme makes its first appearance in Act III, scene 1 as an episode (*The Procurer's Song* b. 103–18) in the set of *Concertante Chorale Variations* between Lulu and the Marquis. The Marquis threatens to inform the police of Lulu's whereabouts if she refuses to accept the job which he has arranged for her in a Cairo brothel. Lulu rejects his offer: 'You can't ask me to sell the only thing I've ever owned – my freedom.' After this the melody disappears (except for a brief distorted reference at b. 491–2 as the Marquis leaves after his argument with the Athlete) until the curtain closes at the end of the first scene, when the orchestra takes up the melody as the basis of the four Variations which form the Interlude.

The first variation of the Interlude (*grandioso*) is in a diatonic C major and in 3/4; the second (*grazioso*) is bitonal and in 4/4; the third (*funèbre*) is atonal and in 5/4 and the last (*affetuoso*) is a twelve-note variation in 7/4. The set thus progresses in terms of pitch organization from tonal to twelve-note and is arranged metrically in such a way that the notated downbeat constantly moves in relation to the melody itself. From the bright, garish orchestration of the opening *grandioso* variation on which the curtain descends at the end of Act III, scene 1 – an orchestration that imitates the sound of an orchestrion and symbolizes the false glitter of the Parisian casino of the previous scene – the curtain rises at the beginning of Act III, scene 2 to the sound of the barrel organ playing the original Wedekind theme in the street below Lulu's London attic. It is, of course, bitterly ironical that the Wedekind theme that was first heard as Lulu refused to submit to the Marquis's attempts to blackmail her into taking a job in a Cairo brothel now forms the backbone of the final scene, in which she is reduced to walking the streets as a common prostitute.

In its simplest form the theme is heard played on the barrel organ at two points in the scene – as the curtain first rises (b. 737–52) and again (b. 826–42) when Lulu is off-stage with her first client.

Variation II, the *grazioso* bitonal variation, returns at b. 1024, as Alwa and Schigolch discuss Lulu's life as a street walker.

The *funèbre* Variation III returns at b. 1110–12, as Schigolch bends over the dead body of Alwa.

Variation IV (*affetuoso*) returns at b. 1008–16 at the end of the Quartet as Lulu prepares to return to the street.

Like *Wozzeck*, *Lulu* also employs an intricate leitmotif system. As in the earlier opera, themes that have initially appeared, and acquired extra-musical associations within the context of the separate numbers of the large-scale forms discussed above, are then employed as independent leitmotifs. The themes of the different parts of Dr Schön's Sonata movement or the main theme of Alwa's Rondo, for example, act as such independent leitmotifs throughout the opera; the theme of the *Canzonetta*, which Lulu sings over the dead body of the Medical Specialist in Act I, scene 1, returns at the death of the Painter in Act I, scene 2 (b. 868–71), the death of Schön in Act II, scene 1 (b. 610–12) and the death of Alwa in Act III, scene 2 (b. 1105–7.) Similarly, a fragment of the Introduction to the *Canon* between Lulu and the Painter in Act I, scene 1 (b. 134–5) returns when the Countess Geschwitz asks, in Act II, scene 1 (b. 28–30), about the artist who painted the portrait.

As important as these melodic leitmotifs, whose dramatic significance springs from the associations which they acquire from the specific textual context in which they first appear, are the harmonic, thematic and rhythmic patterns that are associated with particular characters or objects. In *Lulu*, the note rows, timbres, rhythms and metres – that is to say, every aspect of the music – act as leitmotifs. The way in which these basic musical elements together form the musical language of *Lulu* will be discussed in the following chapter.

6 *Melodic, harmonic and rhythmic language*

Although *Lulu* is a twelve-note work, Berg's handling of the twelve-note method in this, as in his other works, is highly individual. The individuality of Berg's serial techniques has long been recognized but has frequently been misunderstood, many writers choosing to assume that 'Berg uses the twelve-note system only as far as it suits him'[1] and that the emotional impact of Berg's music thus in some way results from his supposedly 'free' handling of the Schoenbergian system. These assumptions are incorrect; Berg's handling of the twelve-note system is not 'free', if by that is meant that Berg uses the method unsystematically or arbitrarily.

In *Lulu* Berg uses a number of different twelve-note rows or sets, most of which are associated with particular characters in the opera. The twelve-note sets of *Lulu* thus function as leitmotifs. Some of these sets are conventional note-rows defined, as in the music of Schoenberg or Webern, by interval sequence, that is to say by the order by which the notes appear in the row. Others, as we shall see, are handled less conventionally. Some of these less conventional sets are regarded as being made up of a number of segments within which the order of the notes, but not of the segments, can be changed. For example, a twelve-note set that was consistently split into three four-note segments thus:

Segment:	A	B	C
Notes	1,2,3,4	5,6,7,8	9,10,11,12

might be presented with the notes permuted like this

Segment:	A	B	C
Notes	4,2,3,1	6,7,8,5	12,11,10,9

or in any other permutation that maintains the identity of the three segments A, B, and C. I shall call such sets 'tropes'. In other segmented sets, the order of the segments, but not the order of the

67

notes within the segments, can be changed. I shall call such sets 'serial tropes'.

Ex. 7

Basic Set

The Basic Set of the whole opera, and one of the few sets not specifically associated with any one character or object (although it frequently represents Lulu herself) is shown in Ex. 7. The Basic Set is unique amongst the sets of *Lulu* in having the ability to reproduce itself in the way demonstrated in Ex. 8. In this example (a) shows the most important or prime form of the set (which I shall call 'P') at its main pitch level '0';[2] (b) shows the same form beginning on the note F sharp, that is, transposed up a tritone (P6); and (c) shows the inverted form (I) of the Basic Set beginning on the note D sharp. As a straightforward transposition of the Basic Set, Ex. 8 (b), of course, maintains the interval sequence of the original in Ex. 8 (a); as an equally straightforward inversion Ex. 8 (c), of course, inverts the interval sequence of the original.

Ex. 8

(a)

(b)

(c)

As the example demonstrates, however, none of the first six notes (the notes of the first hexachord) of Exx. 8 (b) and (c) appears in the first hexachord of Ex. 8 (a). That is to say that all three forms of the row shown in Ex. 8 maintain the distinction between the two harmonic areas defined by the two halves of the Basic Set, harmonic areas that can be most simply expressed in terms of the two chords 'V' and 'W' in Ex. 9. It is perhaps simplest

Ex. 9

V   W

to refer to these two harmonic areas in terms of the piano keyboard and regard them as 'white–' and 'black-note' blocks. As we shall see, the distinction between such 'white' and 'black' note-areas is an important element in the musical language of the opera. In the form shown in Ex. 10, in which the series is systematically divided into three-note segments (1,2,3/4,5,6/7,8,9/10,11,12) and the three-note groups played as chords, the Basic Series is the source of an important harmonic set associated with the portrait of Lulu that we see being painted in the opening scene and that appears in every subsequent scene of the opera. Since these 'Picture chords' result from this particular method of segmenting the Basic Set they, too, maintain the division between the two harmonic areas discussed above.

Ex. 10

Related to, but not identical with, the contrasting white- and black-note blocks defined by the two hexachords of the Basic Set and shown in Exx. 7 and 8 above are the two harmonic areas that link most of the other twelve-note sets in the opera, areas that can be most simply expressed in terms of the two chords (X and Y) shown in Ex. 11.

Ex. 11

Ex. 12 below shows five such harmonically related sets:

(a) the note row associated with Alwa at its most important pitch (beginning with an A minor chord) and with the characteristic contour which provides the main theme of the Rondo of Act II;

(b) the series associated with the Athlete;

(c) the trope associated with the Countess Geschwitz (segment A of which is usually presented as a sustained two-note chord against which are stated segments B and C);

(d) the ordered set associated with the Countess, a series which, although it appears briefly at a few points in Act II, grows in importance as the Countess herself develops into one of the main figures in the work and only becomes an important element in the musical structure in Act III;

(e) the trope, consisting of two chord clusters, associated with the Athlete.

The Athlete's series in Ex. 12 (b) has been permuted to begin on note 10 (a kind of permutation that is a common feature of Berg's twelve-note technique) to demonstrate how it relates to the two harmonic areas (X and Y) shown in Ex. 11. Sets (c), (d) and (e) in Ex. 12 combine the white note-blocks of Y with the additional white note of the first hexachord of the Basic Set. Thus, together, segments A and B of the Countess's trope (c) include all seven white notes. The series associated with the Countess ((d) in Ex. 12) is, like the trope, usually presented as a sustained two-note chord against which are presented the remaining ten notes in sequence. At the pitch level shown in Ex. 12 the last five notes of her set are identical with segment B of her trope and, together with the sustained G-D, cover all seven white notes. The first cluster of the Athlete's trope (e) also covers all seven white notes.

Ex. 12

(a)

Alwa's series (P–0)

(b)

Athlete's series (P–0)

(c)

A   B   C
Countess' trope

(d)

Countess' series

(e)

Athlete's trope

In its most distinctive form (the form in which it appears as the main theme of the Sonata movement in Act I) and at its most important pitch level (P–0), the twelve-note set associated with Dr Schön bears little relation to the common harmonic areas that link the sets shown in Ex. 12, its most noticeable feature being the characteristic A major (as opposed to the A minor of Alwa's set) with which it opens. But although the prime form of Schön's set is

Ex. 13

Dr Schön's series (P–0)

harmonically distinct from the other rows discussed – which is to say that the prime form of the set cannot be transposed to a level at which its two hexachords can be stated as the two chords of Ex. 11 – the *inversion* yields the same harmonic areas as those sets shown in Ex. 12. It is through its inversion that Schön's set relates to most of the other sets of the opera.

Ex. 14

Dr Schön's series (I–0)

As we have seen, neither Schön's series at I–0 nor Alwa's set at P–0 have hexachords that reproduce exactly the content of the Basic Set at P–0. There are no transpositions and no forms of either set the hexachords of which can be reduced to the harmonic areas V and W of Ex. 9. The form of Alwa's set shown in Ex. 12 (a) and of Schön's set shown in Ex. 14, both of which have five notes of each hexachord in common with those of the Basic Set at P–0, are the closest these two sets come to reproducing the harmonic areas of Ex. 9.

The relationships between the different series discussed above thus produce two distinct but related pairs of harmonic blocks: the pair shown in the chords of Ex. 9, which we have called 'V' and 'W' and the pair shown in the chords of Ex. 11 ('X' and 'Y'). The exploitation of these harmonic areas and of the relationships between them has the largest possible influence on the overall structure of the opera.

Ex. 15

The white/black-note opposition which characterizes the sets discussed above is also carried over into some of the other important musical material of the work. Thus, the five-note collection of Ex. 15, embodied in some way in all of the different sets of Ex. 12, acts as an important independent musical idea throughout the opera. This collection, which we shall henceforth call Basic Cell II, is embodied in the first hexachord of Alwa's set at P–0, the first hexachord of Schön's set at I–0, in the 'white note' cluster of the Athlete's trope and in segment B of the Countess's trope. Equally important is the fact that while the first five notes of Schön's row at I–0 consist of a reordered version of Basic Cell II at its main ('white note') pitch level, the second five notes consist of a similarly unordered statement of the inversion of the same cell:

Ex. 16

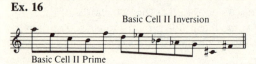

Basic Cell II is one of a number of such short, independent musical ideas in *Lulu* – ideas that permeate the work but are not associated with particular characters or events. Basic Cell II is second in importance only to what I shall call Basic Cell I, the figure shown in Ex. 17, which is, perhaps, the most important idea in the whole opera:

Ex. 17

Ex. 17 shows Basic Cell I at its most important pitch level, on the notes Bb–Eb–E–A, a pitch at which it contains in microcosm the white/black note opposition of the sets discussed above. It is at this level that, announced *forte* by the trombone, the cell is heard as the opening notes of the work, that it appears in the central 'Film Music' Interlude and that it dominates the final scene of the opera. Like the Basic Set, Basic Cell I has certain unique properties which make it peculiarly well suited to the important role assigned to it in the opera, most notably, in this case, its symmetrical structure and its identity as two interlocking tritones. The consequences of these features are:

(1) a tritone transposition of any form of the cell reproduces all the notes of the original (that is, in the case of Ex. 17 the transposition beginning on E shown in Ex. 18 (a));

(2) an inversion of the cell a fourth above or a semitone lower also reproduces all the notes of the original (in the case of Ex. 17 the inversions beginning on A and Eb shown in Exx. 18 (b) and (c));

(3) the cell has no independent retrograde form, its retrograde being identical with its inversion, a feature that is especially exploited in the palindromic Film Music between the two scenes of Act II (see Ex. 18).

Ex. 18

All of the sets illustrated earlier in this chapter have embodied in them an ordered version of Basic Cell I. Both Alwa's set and Schön's set, for example, include ordered versions of Basic Cell I, at its most important level, as demonstrated by the stemmed notes in Ex. 19. Naturally, the statements of this cell embodied in the

Ex. 19

twelve-note sets maintain all those properties of Basic Cell I that have already been discussed above. The tritone transposition of Schön's set, for example, simply changes over the position of the two fourths which form Basic Cell I (as shown in Ex. 20).

Ex. 20

Similarly, since the sustained dyad of the Countess's ordered set (Ex. 12 (d)) consists of a perfect fifth, juxtaposed tritone transpositions of this set also produce statements of Basic Cell I (see Ex. 21).

Ex. 21

A few sets stand outside this network of harmonic relationships. Most of these sets are associated with less important figures in the work – the Medical Specialist (and his 'doubles' the Banker and the First Client), the Painter and the Schoolboy. The Medical Specialist's set is shown in Ex. 22 (a). It is derived directly from the Basic Set of the opera, two notes of which are extracted and sustained while the remaining notes are played as two-note chords. The Painter is represented by the series of two-note chords shown in Ex. 22 (b), which are produced by playing the two hexachords of the Basic Set simultaneously. The sequence of four-note chords shown in Ex. 22 (c), an important element in the harmonic structure of the opera, is produced by playing the dyads of Ex. 22 (b) in pairs. The Schoolboy is represented by the set shown in Ex. 22 (d).

Ex. 22

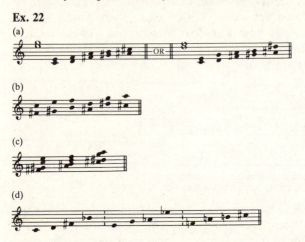

The most important of the sets that stand outside the network of harmonic relationships described above is the set associated with the figure of Schigolch, the old beggar who shares with Lulu (and who symbolizes) her mysterious past. Schigolch, the only character in the opera to accept Lulu for what she is and call her by her real name, is the only one of the main characters to survive at the end of the work. In keeping with his role as the symbol of Lulu's mythological origins, Schigolch is represented by a set which, as Perle has pointed out[3] symbolizes the ultimate origin of all the music in the opera – a segmented set the three segments of which consist of differently ordered fragments of the chromatic scale (see Ex. 23).

Ex. 23

Two other sets stand outside the main network of harmonic relationships: the first is the scale-like pattern associated with the figure of Lulu herself, a set (shown in Ex. 24 (a)) that, derived from the picture chords of Ex. 10, appears only as a melodic figuration. The second, the set shown in Ex. 24 (b), is associated with the triple-role of the Prince, Manservant and the Marquis.

Ex. 24
(a)

(b)

In addition to the two Basic Cells discussed earlier, three other Basic Cells are worthy of mention:

(i) Basic Cell III, shown in Ex. 25 (a), is a diminished seventh chord, a chord which, like Basic Cell I, is symmetrical and therefore non-invertible and non-retrogradable. Three successive statements of this diminished chord, each a semitone higher than the one before, will produce all twelve notes of the chromatic scale;

(ii) Basic Cell IV shown in Ex. 25 (b), which (often heard on the vibraphone in imitation of the doorbell and often linked to the diminished seventh of Basic Cell III) marks important exits and entrances in the work and which always appears at the pitch shown in the example:

(iii) Basic Cell V, the rhythmic cell shown in Ex. 25 (c). Statements of this rhythmic cell, which functions as a 'fate rhythm' throughout the opera, underline every important event in the opera. Some (but not all) appearances of the 'fate rhythm' are marked in the score by the symbol 'RH' standing for *Hauptrhythmus*.

Ex. 25
(a)

(b)

(c)

The death of the Painter in Act I, scene 2 is accompanied by a five-part rhythmic canon on the 'fate rhythm' played by unpitched percussion (a canon which is itself part of a much larger rhythmic structure, the *Monoritmica*, based entirely on the same *Hauptrhythmus*); the deaths of Schön and later of Countess Geschwitz are similarly marked by successive statements of the rhythm. Lulu's final cries of 'Nein, nein, nein, nein' before her death scream are set to the same rhythm. The end and beginning of each act are similarly marked – the end of Act I and the opening of Act II by repeated statements of Schön's A major chord in the *Hauptrhythmus*, the end of Act II and (in the guise of a repeat of the circus music from the Prologue) the beginning of Act III by repeated RH statements of the A minor chord associated with Alwa, the end of Act III by statements of both Schön's and Alwa's chords, as well as the white-note segment B from Countess Geschwitz's trope, in the same rhythm. Although every important event (and almost every important sentence) in the work is underlined by appearances of this 'fate rhythm', only one theme in the opera – that of the Coda of Dr Schön's Act I Sonata movement – is consistently associated with this rhythm. It is, as we have said, an association that, initially expressing Dr Schön's fatal inability to break his ties with Lulu, acquires a new and ironic significance as the same music returns on the entry of Schön's Doppelgänger, Jack.

A feature of *Lulu* is the extent to which all the different aspects of the musical language – rhythm, metre and timbre as well as pitch – are involved in the leitmotivic structure of the piece. In addition to the 'fate rhythm' shown above, which has a general rather than personal significance, specific rhythmic leitmotifs are associated with the figures of the Medical Specialist and, more importantly, the Countess Geschwitz. The Medical Specialist's rhythm (which is obviously related to the 'fate rhythm' and indeed functions as such since the Medical Specialist dies within a few moments of his first appearance on stage) is shown in Ex. 26 (a). The melodrama which accompanies his death in Act I, scene 1 is an ostinato based on statements of this rhythm. More important is the kind of *accelerando–ritardando* rhythmic pattern shown in Ex. 26 (b) which is associated with the figure of the Countess Geschwitz and which, becoming (like her ordered set) more and more important as the opera progresses and the Countess herself grows in stature, acts as a true leitmotif – a rhythmic leitmotif as important as the pitch motifs (the trope and set) associated with this character.

Ex. 26

(a)

(b)

The rhythmic structure of the vocal part of the Countess's Nocturno in Act III, scene 2 is built entirely of repeated statements of this rhythmic motif while the section following Lulu's death cry, as the Countess rushes to her help, is completely dominated by it. A special variant of the 'fate rhythm', one which incorporates the characteristic accelerando pattern, is associated with the Countess:

Ex. 27

Numerous other ingenious and highly individual techniques for organizing rhythm, metre and temp can be found throughout *Lulu*.[4] In some cases these techniques operate mainly within the confines of individual numbers. The rhythmic structure of Schön's 'Das mein Lebensabend' in Act II, scene 1 provides an example. In this number the instrumental parts are based on two repeating 'isorhythms': two rhythmic ostinati, one of which determines the rhythmic patterns of the opening and closing sections of the number, whilst the other determines the rhythmic patterns that appear in the central section. The first isorhythm consists of six separate note-values, the second of eight (Ex. 28) but, since these rhythms are applied to a pitch-sequence of seven notes (the last seven notes of the inversion of Schön's row) the relationship between the pitch and the durational series constantly changes. Since, moreover, the first isorhythm has a total length of twelve semiquavers and the second a total of fifteen semiquavers and the number is notated in 4/4 (that is to say that there are sixteen semiquavers in each bar) the two isorhythms constantly change their position in relation to the bar line, as well as in relation to the seven-note pitch-sequence. The setting up of repeating rhythmic figurations which constantly shift in relation to the metric accents in this way is a common feature of Berg's music; the three ensembles of Act III, scene 1 of *Lulu* provide other examples of such shifting ostinati.

Ex. 28

In contrast to these examples, in which repeated rhythmic patterns move against a fixed metre, the orchestral *Variations*

Interlude between the two scenes of Act III shows Berg exploring the possibilities of shifting the metric accent as a means of varying a melody that has a regular and predictable periodic and rhythmic structure. In this Interlude, although the melody and the rhythm of the Wedekind *Lautenlied* remain unchanged throughout, the tune changes its position in relation to the bar line from one statement to the next as the length of the bar extends from 3 to 4, 5, 7 and eventually 10 crotchets with each variation.

Against such techniques, which are mainly of local significance, must be set Berg's use of interrelated tempi and mathematically related metronome marks to organize large sections of music. In *Lulu* the tempi of whole scenes (and sometimes of even larger spans) are frequently related in this way, with the result that the tempi both articulate the main musical and dramatic structure and weld the individual numbers into larger and more cohesive units. The tempo-structure of Act III, scene 1 – which rests on the three big ensembles which dominate the scene – shows the technique in its clearest possible form; the three ensembles use related musical material and have metronome markings of crotchet = 90, 60 and 120, respectively. Other scenes, such as Act II, scene 1 and Act III, scene 2 have more complicated tempi structures.

The most famous example in *Lulu* of the use of interrelated tempi appears in the *Monoritmica* of Act I, scene 2. The first half of the *Monoritmica* consists of seven sections with tempi markings which gradually increase from quaver = 76 to quaver = 132, six sections with tempi increasing from crotchet = 76 (that is, double the speed of the original tempo) to crotchet = 132 and five sections increasing in tempo from minim. = 76 to minim. = 132. Not only does the tempo gradually and systematically increase throughout these first eighteen sections but the rate of increase itself grows large (describing, as it were, an exponential curve) as the difference between one tempo and the next becomes progressively greater towards the central point of the *Monoritmica*. The second half then reverses the tempo sequence of the first. The individual rhythmic patterns which appear within this larger tempo structure are themselves determined by the *Hauptrhythmus*.

Like those of the *Monoritmica*, the metronome markings (and many other aspects) of the Prologue also define an overall palindromic progression, moving from crotchet = 80–90 at the opening, through a series of mathematically related tempi to a central crotchet = 40 and then back again to crotchet = 90–80 at the end.

Perhaps the most important and extensive example of Berg's use of interrelated tempi in *Lulu* occurs in Act I where the tempi from the moment of Schön's entry in Act I, scene 2 to the final bars of scene 3 are linked in this way; a span of almost a thousand bars of music that includes not only the *Monoritmica* but also the whole of Schön's Sonata movement. The Sonata movement itself is particularly interesting, since here Berg not only employs mathematically related tempi but shows the way in which one tempo evolves from another. Such 'metric modulations', effected by introducing into the original tempo a syncopation which then becomes the basic pulse of the new tempo – are particularly evident in the Sonata development section. Since, in such cases, the relationship between the two different tempi can be expressed by notating both in a single common tempo, the device also offers the composer the opportunity of superimposing and employing different time layers simultaneously. An example of such superimposition of different tempi appears in the *Gavotte* section of the final Sonata reprise when the material of the *Gavotte*, moving at its original tempo of crotchet = 69 is accompanied by repeated statements of the fateful Sonata Coda theme, notated in such a way that the Coda theme is, in effect, moving at a tempo of crotchet = 46, the speed at which it will later appear in the final bars of the act.

While the Countess is associated with a specific rhythmic pattern, three other characters – Schigolch, the Athlete and the Schoolboy – are often associated with metric patterns. Although it is an association that is less consistent than is the Countess's association with the rythmic pattern discussed above (and it is certainly less consistent than is their own association with individual twelve-note sets) it is particularly noticeable in Act II, where these three characters appear together. In these passages Schigolch's part is usually notated in 2/4 or 4/4, the Athlete's in 6/4 or 6/8 and the Schoolboy's in 9/8 or 12/8. The same associations are maintained in Act III, where the conversations between Lulu and Schigolch and between Lulu and the Athlete are in 2/4 and 6/8 respectively. At the point at which, in the Prologue, the Athlete is identified as 'the bear' the metre changes to the Athlete's 6/8.

Finally the Athlete, Schigolch and the Schoolboy are also associated with particular instrumental timbres in the part of Act II, scene 1 in which they appear together on stage – Schigolch with a chamber group consisting of solo low strings (the figure of Schigolch is consistently associated with a chamber ensemble throughout the work; his first entry in Act I, scene 2 is marked by the beginning of a nonet for wind), the Schoolboy with wind and the Athlete with brass and percussion. More noticeable, however – and maintained throughout the opera – is the association of the Athlete with the piano (most obviously in the characteristic presentation of his trope as piano chord clusters) and the association of the triple role of the Prince/Manservant/Marquis with solo strings: the Prince in Act I, scene 3 with a solo cello; the Manservant in Act II, scene 1 with a solo viola and the Marquis in Act III, scene 1 with the solo violin. When, in the Prologue, the Animal Trainer, using the Marquis's row, mentions the 'amusing little monkey' his reference is accompanied by string figurations which, beginning on the solo double bass, gradually ascend to the solo cello, the solo viola and finally the solo violin. The final outcome of these timbral associations is the double *Cadenza* for solo violin and piano which accompanies the discussion between the Athlete and the Marquis in Act III, scene 1.

It is impossible in the confines of the present book to give anything more than a general catalogue of the basic material of the opera. Berg's handling of this material – his understanding of the ramifications of its structural potential, the subtlety with which he bends it to his overall purposes and the dramatic and musical skill with which he relates the different sets – is so rich that it would itself require a separate book to begin to do it justice.[5] The following chapter will, however, try to give some indication of the way in which this raw material is handled by examining one short passage of the opera.

7 Act III, scene 2, b. 1146–1326: an analysis

The last 150 bars of *Lulu*, the moment when Jack and Lulu finally confront one another and the subsequent death of Countess Geschwitz, are the emotional and dramatic focus of the whole opera. The music to which Berg set his closing scene – a music that embodies all his humanity and sympathy for the poor creatures who people his opera – must be amongst the most purely beautiful written by any composer this century. It is through the sheer power of this music that Berg, like Mozart with his setting of the Countess's words of forgiveness at the end of *Figaro*, transforms the text – in this case the sordid haggling over the amount which a client will pay a prostitute – into something overwhelmingly moving and something which, in retrospect, changes our view of the whole work.

The emotional and dramatic effect of these final bars is complex and highly ambiguous, and I shall discuss their larger significance, and their effect on our understanding of the work as a whole, in the final chapter. The present chapter will primarily be concerned with showing how, in these 150 bars, the building blocks described in chapter 5 are put together to form a musical and dramatic whole.

Here, as in the rest of the opera, the specific musical material employed at any point is that associated with the characters on stage or involved in the action at the time. The other important elements determining the large-scale organization of this final 'scena' are the basic cells discussed in chapter 5 and, in particular:

(a) the 'fate rhythm' of Basic Cell V and the variant associated with Countess Geschwitz (Ex. 29 (a) and (b)).

Ex. 29

(a)   (b)

(b) the diminished seventh chord of Basic Cell III, the minor thirds of which are reflected in many of the progressions of the base line and determine the pitch of many of the sets used during the passage;

81

(c) the white-note collection of Basic Cell II (Ex, 30), which is identical in content with one segment of the Countess's trope and with the first five notes of Schön's row at I–0;

Ex. 30

(d) the notes and structure of Basic Cell I especially at the transposition (P–0) shown in Ex. 31.

Ex. 31

It was at this, its main transposition level (on the notes E–A/Bb–Eb) that Basic Cell I was heard as the opening notes of the Prologue at the very beginning of the opera, that it appeared as a constantly repeated figuration in the Film Music Interlude at the centre of the work and that it now dominates the final moments of the piece. The structural importance of Basic Cell I in the present scene lies particularly in

(i) its appearance as the opening notes of the two hexachords of Schön's note row at P–0 and I–0 (Ex. 32), two forms that become especially prominent during the final scene as the appearance of Jack initiates a reprise of the material associated with his double Dr. Schön, and

Ex. 32

(ii) the relationship between the Cell and the material associated with the Countess Geschwitz, a relationship that is only fully revealed in this final scene of the opera.

All those moments towards the end of the scene at which the Countess becomes the main protagonist in the drama are marked *either*

(a) by statements of her ordered series at transpositions at which successive statements of the sustained perfect fifth segment of her set produce the notes of Basic Cell I at the level shown in Ex. 31 (thus, for example, both the *Andante* section at b. 1175 and the final *Grave* section at b. 1315 begin with successive statements of the two forms shown in Ex. 33, in which the fifths of Basic Cell I are indicated by dotted beams).

Ex. 33
III/2 b.1175
Andante

or

(b) statements of her trope or series at transpositions a minor third apart, so that the top and bottom lines of successive sustained fifths form the diminished seventh chord of Basic Cell III (while the fifths of alternate statements form Basic Cell I); Ex. 34 illustrates this through a schematic version of the opening of the Countess's *Nocturno* at b. 1279;

Ex. 34

III/2 b.1279
(I)

or

(c) figurations that exploit the relationship between Basic Cell I and the symmetrical patterns that are consistently associated with Countess Geschwitz throughout the opera. The relation between these inversional patterns and Basic Cell I can be seen at the Countess's first entrance in the last scene of the opera (b. 888 *et seq.*) when P– and I– statements of her trope, beginning four-and-a-half octaves apart on the A–E fifth of Basic Cell I, gradually converge to meet on the other, Bb–Eb, fifth of the cell and then, continuing their convergence, finally meet again on the A–E (although now a unison) from which the progression started. Ex. 35 shows this passage in diagramatic form.

Ex. 35
III/2 b.888

Other, similar, symmetrical formations permeate the whole of the final passage and will be pointed out at the relevant points in the following analysis.

As Schigolch makes his final exit and the Countess Geschwitz is left alone on stage, there begins (b. 1146–74) a darkly scored *Sostenuto* (the music that opens the final movement of the *Symphonic Pieces from 'Lulu'*) as the Countess contemplates suicide as a way of touching Lulu's feelings. The music of the *Sostenuto* alternates short units based on the Countess's trope (b. 1146–50; 1156–9; 1164–6; 1170–4) with those based on her ordered series. Against a single held octave Ab on oboe and cor anglais, and supported by a soft roll on the bass drum, the lower wind and strings present two forms of the Countess's trope a fifth apart as ascending and descending sequences of parallel perfect fifths. The rhythm of the ascending (on bassoon and double bassoon) and descending fifths (on cellos and double basses) together produce the characteristic *accelerando–ritardando* pattern associated with the Countess. The final perfect fifth of each sequence is prolonged, and the two become the sustained fifth of the following statement of the Countess's series (Ex. 36). Over the passage as a whole the progression of sustained bass fifths outlines the diminished seventh of Basic Cell III.

Ex. 36

III/2 b. 1146

Like every other section in this final scene the *Sostenuto* forms part of a large-scale composed *ritardando*. From this point onwards the tempi of successive sections slow down from the crotchet = 67 (*Andante* b. 1175), crotchet = 58 (*Adagio* b. 1188), crotchet = 52 (*Lento* b. 1279), crotchet = 46 (*Largo* b. 1292) and finally to crotchet = 42 (*Grave* b. 1315).

Recognizing that suicide would be a futile gesture ('She wouldn't weep a tear for me') the Countess moves towards Lulu's portrait; as she does so there unfolds in the strings, for the first time (b. 1174 *et seq.*), the full lyrical, melodic form of her ordered series, the form that will return in the voice as the melody of her final *Liebestod*. The melody consists of two statements of her series at a level (the transpositions shown in Ex. 33 above) at which the sustained open fifths, now transformed into a gently rocking figuration in the bass, form the notes of Basic Cell I at its main pitch level on E, A, Bb, Eb. As the Countess sinks to her knees to make a final appeal to Lulu's portrait (b. 1180 'Have pity on me') converging statements of the portrait chords,[1] again in the Countess's characteristic *accelerando–ritardando* rhythmic pattern, gradually come to rest on the Eb–Bb of Basic Cell I. These two notes are sustained against an oscillating figuration around three chromatic notes on the clarinet as the opening phrase of the first subject of Schön's Sonata movement (the opening E–A of the Sonata theme forming a statement of Basic Cell I with the sustained Eb–Bb) announces the entrance of Lulu and Jack.

The significance of the chromatic oscillation becomes clear as Jack pauses to look at Geschwitz. 'Who is that?' he asks. 'My sister', replies Lulu, 'she's mad.' As George Perle has pointed out,[2] the chromatic oscillating figure has appeared earlier in the opera, at the end of Schön's 'Das mein Lebensabend' as the setting of Schön's words 'Insanity [*Irrsinn*] has taken possession of my reason'; it now returns in response to the appearance of the word 'mad' (*verrückt*) in the text. 'Mad?' replies Jack (to a softly arpeggiated version of Basic Cell I), lost in thought as he contemplates Lulu's reply. The stage direction that he be *in Gedanken* appears in the score at the precise moment when Lulu says the word *verrückt*. There is, as Perle has observed:

a characteristically Bergian touch of irony here in the seemingly coincidental reference of the leitmotif to the Countess's supposed 'insanity' for it is, of course, Jack, not Geschwitz, who is the personification of Dr Schön's *Irrsinn*. Perhaps also the approximately five seconds, a long time in the given musical and dramatic context, that Jack is to remain *in Gedanken* is meant to establish a somewhat emphatic relation between Jack and the

Countess, two human beings condemned by fate to an obsessive deviation from normal sexuality that isolates them from their fellow creatures.[3]

As Jack turns away from Geschwitz to Lulu ('You seem to have a pretty mouth') the chromatic oscillation slows down and disappears, and the Coda theme of Schön's Sonata movement makes its first, an initially brief, reappearance (b. 1193–9). A semitone higher than on its original appearance, the theme will return to its original pitch and be fully reprised only on its final appearance in the scene. 'How much do you want?' asks Jack. 'Won't you stay the whole night?' replies Lulu. Berg has here modified Wedekind's text to make the form of Lulu's asking Jack to stay ('Wollen Sie denn nicht die ganze Nacht hier bleiben?') correspond to that of her begging Schön to spend the afternoon with her in Act II, scene 1 ('Könnest Du Dich für heute nachmittag nicht frei lassen?'). Her question to Jack initiates a reprise (b. 1219 *et seq*) of the earlier music, the *Cavatina* from Act II, scene 1. The previous domestic quarrel between Lulu and Schön, to which this music first appeared, now finds a grotesque and blackly ironic parallel in the sordid haggling between Lulu and Schön's double.

To a vocal part that superimposes gently moving triplets on to the seductive tango rhythm of the *Cavatina*, Lulu attempts to persuade Jack to stay; he answers in curt, business-like and rhythmically stilted recitative phrases. 'How much do you want', repeats Jack 'I don't have much money.' 'I'm not asking for gold nuggets', replies Lulu, 'only for a little something.' The music of the earlier *Cavatina* is interrupted as Jack turns to leave. 'For God's sake stay', pleads Lulu. 'Why should I . . . it sounds suspicious . . . someone will go through my pockets while I'm asleep', replies Jack to the music of Schön's 'Das mein Lebensabend' from Act II; the music to which Schön originally voiced his disgust with the people around him and his fear for his life. As on its earlier appearance, the white-note collection of Basic Cell II (the first five notes of Schön's row at I–0) is played as a repeated chord in the 'fate rhythm' while horizontal versions of the same notes form the vocal lines – Jack's 'Guten Abend' and, in the characteristic form associated with Basic Cell II, Lulu's subsequent replies. The A–E dyad of Basic Cell I embodied in this white-noted collection is complemented by the remaining E♭–B♭ which appears prominently in both the vocal part and the accompanying isorhythmic bassoon figuration. 'Give me half what I asked for', says Lulu returning to the music of the

Cavatina. 'No, that's too much', says Jack and then, momentarily abandoning his brusque attitude, lapses for the only time into the tango rhythm of the *Cavatina.* 'You don't seem to have been at this for very long.' 'Today is the first time', says Lulu to a statement of Basic Cell I at P–0.

The converging statements of the portrait chords in the Countess's *accelerando-ritardando* rhythm reappear as Countess Geschwitz, who, ignored by both Lulu and Jack, has remained kneeling before the portrait, suddenly half-rises and reaches towards Jack (b. 1230). 'Will you be still', says Lulu, irritated. 'That isn't your sister', observes Jack to the melodic form of the Countess's series (it is the only time in the opera that her series is sung by anyone other than herself), 'the poor creature is in love with you!' In what Perle has called one of the most poignant moments in both the play and the opera, Jack reaches over to Geschwitz and strokes her hair 'as if she were a dog', expressing 'a note of understanding for Geschwitz that no one else . . . ever expresses'.[4] As Jack again turns from Geschwitz to Lulu, soft descending versions of the Countess's trope lead (b. 1235–61) to a final recapitulation of the Sonata Coda material at its original pitch and in the extended form in which it originally appeared as the orchestral interlude between Act I, scenes 2 and 3.

The haggling between Lulu and Jack now continues to the accompaniment of the rich, Mahlerian Coda theme, a theme that brings with it from its earlier appearances a host of associations. On its earlier appearances the Sonata Coda theme has not only symbolized Schön's and Lulu's love for each other but has also, as the only theme in the whole work whose rhythmic structure consists entirely of repeated statements of the *Hauptrhythmus*, symbolized Schön's weakness and his fatal inability to break free of Lulu. The repeated statements of the 'fate rhythm' built into the Coda theme now acquire a new significance – both ironic and deeply moving – as they anticipate the form which this final breaking-free will take.

As the central section of the Coda material closes, Jack and Lulu leave for the room in which she will be murdered. Lulu turns to pick up a lamp. 'We don't need a lamp, the moon is shining', says Jack and, as he does so, the final syllable of his vocal line moves up a semitone (b. 1259) from E to a high F natural to form the third of the Db major chord that now begins the final restatement of the main Coda theme. With the memory of Lulu's words from the second *Intermezzo* of the previous scene in mind ('I can tell in the darkest night when a man is right for me'), and remembering both that Lulu has pleaded with Jack to stay and that she had earlier described Schön, Jack's alter ego, as the only man she has ever loved, the effect of this musical resolution is overpowering and its implications deeply disturbing. Here, as throughout this final scene between Lulu and Jack, the juxtaposition of the luxuriant musical material and the sordid stage action, coupled with the complexity of the associations called up, gives the scene extraordinary emotional and dramatic resonance.

To a climactic version of the music to which she first appeared in the Prologue of the opera, Lulu makes her final exit with Jack. The sustained Eb–Bb returns with the 'insanity' clarinet oscillation which preceded Jack's entrance (b. 1277), the clarinet figuration dies away and the sustained Eb-Bb is joined by the remaining A–E of Basic Cell I as Countess Geschwitz, alone once more, sings a soft dream-like *Nocturno*.

The *Nocturno* is a number that creates an extraordinary atmosphere in the theatre. Over long sustained bass notes, which outline the descending minor thirds of the diminished seventh of Basic Cell III, the other orchestral parts quietly circle around the notes of the Countess's series, now in fixed immobile groups, to create a gently undulating but almost totally unchanging, undeveloping texture. Above this the voice intones, in the Countess's characteristic *accelerando–ritardando* rhythm, each phrase of the text on a single note. Never rising to a dynamic above piano the whole

Ex. 37

III/2 b. 1279

Das   ist der letz-te   A-bend den ich mit die-sem Volk ver - brin - ge

passage creates a moment of almost total stasis as the whole work stands poised, waiting for the coming violence.

'This is the last evening I shall spend with these people', says Geschwitz. 'I'll go back to Germany. I'll matriculate, study law and fight for women's rights.' The placing of these words immediately before the eruption of the violent act of male destructiveness that follows is particularly telling.

Against a sustained diminished seventh chord ('ppp – like an echo') we hear, to Basic Cell I and in the rhythm of the opera's fateful *Hauptrhythmus*, Lulu's off-stage cry of 'No, no – no, no!'

which is immediately cut off (b. 1294) by the strident fortefortiss-
imo twelve-note chord that accompanies her death-cry. The 'death-
chord' is a vertical arrangement of the three distinct versions of
Basic Cell I that together produce a complete chromatic collection
with the P–0 form (A–E, Bb–Eb) in the bass. As Geschwitz rushes
to the door to help Lulu, the death-chord is systematically dismantled from the bottom upwards. First the Basic Cell I at P–0
component is presented as a sequence of ascending fifths a tritone
apart in the manner shown in Ex. 38.

Ex. 38

The final A–E fifth is prolonged as a shrill, high reiterated
pattern. Presented in this way, both the pitch material (through
being presented as perfect fifths, which associate it with the perfect
fifth segment of the Countess series and trope) and its rhythmic
presentation (with its *accelerando–ritardando* pattern) associate
Basic Cell I with the Countess Geschwitz. As the reiterated pattern
begins to slow down, the second (on G sharp–C sharp/D–G) and
then the third (C–F/F sharp–B) versions of the basic cell in the
death chord are similarly dismantled (b. 1297–9). The six-note
chord resulting from the superimposition of the three perfect fifths
is sustained by a tremolo on high violins and fluttertongued wind.
    The door at which Geschwitz has been beating is suddenly
thrown open by Jack (an action accompanied by a series of savage,
gradually accelerating, chromatic clusters on the brass, achieved by
stating three levels of Schön's row simultaneously) who stabs the
Countess. The last of the three descending chord clusters which
mark the Countess's collapse is identical with the notes of the
'insanity' chromatic oscillation on clarinets earlier in the scene.
'That was a good bit of work', remarks Jack (echoing the words that

Schön used in Act I, scene 2) to a descending statement of Basic Cell I at P–0. Geschwitz's own version of the fateful *Hauptrhythmus* is heard on the bass drum as he walks past her, and the notes of Basic Cell I gradually contract to arrive back at the chromatic *Irrsinn* cluster. 'I'm a lucky fellow', says Jack to the opening bars of Schön's 'Das mein Lebensabend' as he washes his hands and, to a distorted chromatic version of the Prologue's circus music (and with the *Hauptrhythmus* in the bass), searches in vain for a towel. As he leaves, interlocking versions of Basic Cell I a semitone apart (interlocking in that the two forms share the tritone A–E♭) decorate a repetition of the music that accompanied his entrance.

Alone once more, the dying Geschwitz sings her final soliloquy, a *Liebestod* which repeats the material of the earlier *Andante* (b. 1175) and which finally gives way to descending statements of the Countess's trope and Basic Cell I. As George Perle has said 'the three concluding chords of the final act epitomize the fate of the three persons most profoundly involved with Lulu'.[5] The first chord (b. 1324) is the A major chord associated with Dr. Schön, the chord which ended the first and opened the second act and the repetitions of which, then as now, are determined by the rhythm of the *Hauptrhythmus*. In the following bar the C sharp of Schön's chord descends a semitone to produce the A minor triad associated with Alwa which, again in the 'fate rhythm', closed Act II. Finally, as the Countess dies, the C of Alwa's chord descends a further semitone to arrive at B natural and produce, in the last chord of the opera, part of the white-note collection of Basic Cell II which characterizes Geschwitz's trope.

8 *A suggested interpretation*

With a plot the subject-matter of which includes prostitution, blackmail, homosexuality, white-slave traffic, suicide, sex murder and a variety of other unsavoury topics, *Lulu* has a libretto that is undeniably sordid and that many people find distasteful and offensive. Were *Lulu* simply sordid it might, perhaps, be possible to come to terms with its unpleasantness by seeing the piece as a manifestation of the *fin-de-siècle* fascination with decadence, corruption and erotic, violent death that characterizes so much of the literature and visual art of the period (in, for example, the works of Wilde, Poe, Rimbaud, Stefan George, Munch, Beardsley and many other artists). Alternatively, we might understand the opera as belonging to that other group of late nineteenth- and early twentieth-century works that deals, either naturalistically or satirically, with the underside of society, a group to which, in different ways, belong the works of Dostoevsky, Zola, Lautrec, Otto Dix and George Grosz. We might then regard the opera as a piece of social criticism, arguing, as does Hans Redlich in his 1957 book on Berg, that *Lulu* like *Wozzeck* shows Berg's sympathy and compassion for the underdog in society.[1]

But what makes *Lulu* especially disturbing is that the plot is both sordid and absurd. If we are to argue that *Lulu* is a work of social criticism then we must admit that it goes about criticizing society in an unusual way. What are we, sitting in the audience, to make of this strange story with its bizarre mixture of tragedy and farce, a story in which the apparently everyday world is the setting for a series of events that are so ridiculously unbelievable that we can hardly be expected to take the piece seriously?

In *Wozzeck*, the plot moves directly to its goal, omitting everything that is not relevant, and the fate of the main protagonists has the simplicity and inevitability of a Greek tragedy; in the wandering, discursive dramatic structure of *Lulu*, the deaths of the

91

characters (from the heart attack which, in Act I, scene 1, kills the Medical Specialist when he has been on stage for only a few minutes, to the murder of Lulu and Geschwitz in Act III, scene 2) are arbitrary and seem to depend entirely on the whim of the author.

If we are to regard Berg's *Lulu* as being more than what one writer has described as 'a vision of the wilful desecration of mere subhumans at the hands of a gratuitous plot, all imprisoned in a cold, hard musical structure',[2] we must try to explain why Berg chose, and what he wanted to achieve in setting, so apparently absurd, sordid and to many people repulsive a libretto.

In his autobiography Stefan Zweig has left a memorable description of the 'sticky, perfumed, sultry, unhealthy atmosphere'[3] of the Vienna of Berg's day. The Vienna in which Berg was born and lived was a city in which the veneer of respectability hid a sensuality that permeated all classes of society. It was a society in which a man was expected to have affairs but which 'upheld the fiction that a well-brought-up woman neither possessed sexual instincts nor was permitted to possess any as long as she remained unmarried',[4] a society that thrived on a 'morality of secrecy', refusing to recognize openly the sexuality with which it was privately obsessed. 'Just as cities, under the cleanly swept streets with their handsome deluxe shops and elegant promenades hide a system of subterranean sewers which carry their filth, so the entire sexual life was supposed to go on under a moral surface of "society", outside the walls of respectability and "sacred morality".'

The Vienna of the turn-of-the-century had the greatest number of prostitutes of any city in Europe, a 'gigantic army' of prostitutes, a wealth of brothels, 'closed houses' and salons where

there were hidden doors and special stairs by which members of the highest society could pay their visits without being seen by other mortals. There were mirrored rooms and some that offered a hidden view of the neighbouring room; there were the weirdest changes of costumes locked away in chests and closets for particular fetishists.[5]

Even the most respectable restaurants had 'chambres separées', rooms in which couples could eat and amuse themselves in privacy.

And this was the same city, the same society, the same morality that was indignant when young girls rode bicycles and declared it a disgrace to the dignity of science when Freud, in his calm, clear and penetrating manner, established truths that they did not wish to be true. The same world that so pathetically defended the purity of womanhood allowed the cruel sale of women, organized it and even profited thereby.[6]

It is the sexual and moral hypocrisy of this society that is one of the subjects of Berg's opera; a hypocrisy that, despite Zweig's belief that it had been swept away, remains part of our own present-day society. It is a hypocrisy that is symbolized by the fact that each of Lulu's lovers calls her by a different name. Only the old beggar Schigolch, who shares her mythical past, calls Lulu by her real name, accepts her for what she is and survives at the end of the opera. It is a hypocrisy that is also suggested in the opera (although not in the plays) by Berg's use of multiple roles and in particular by his doubling of the roles of Lulu's husbands in the first half of the opera with the roles of Lulu's clients in the final scene. The use of these double and treble roles is both the basis of the musical structure of the work, as we have seen, and one of the keys to its dramatic meaning, for it is through these doublings and the musical symmetries that spring from them that the opera makes its wider point. By having the performers who played Lulu's husbands also play her clients, Berg not only illustrates Karl Kraus' view that the final scene represents the 'revenge of the world of men' for what she has done to them (or, more correctly, for what, because of their refusal to accept reality, they have chosen to do to themselves), but he also illustrates the moral dishonesty of the 'respectable bourgeois society' inhabited by the characters of the earlier scenes. Through this doubling the newspaper magnate, the medical specialist and the artist are equated with the shadowy characters who inhabit the *demi-monde* of the final scenes; the pillars of respectable bourgeois society and the unsavoury inhabitants of the sleazy criminal world are the same – different sides of the same coin.

Throughout the opera we are made aware that what we are seeing on the stage has some relevance to us in the audience. 'Roll up and see my wild animals', says the Animal Trainer at the beginning of the Prologue, 'real wild animals, not tame domesticated ones like those in the stalls.' It is a simile that is taken up again in Act II, scene 1 – the crucial scene set in Lulu's back-stage dressing room at the cabaret theatre – as Alwa's soliloquy is interrupted by the cheers of the off-stage audience watching Lulu's cabaret performance. We, the domesticated and respectable audience in the opera house are here confronted with a reflection, a mirror-image, of ourselves. 'They sound like animals in the menagerie at feeding time', comments Alwa contemptuously as he listens to the cheers of the back-stage audience.

In *Lulu* Berg is attempting something very different from what he attempted in *Wozzeck* and far more difficult to achieve. *Wozzeck* is an expressionist opera, the whole dramatic force of which comes from the fact that we are forced to see everything that happens through the eyes of Wozzeck himself. The world of *Wozzeck* – a world, peopled by grotesques, in which even natural phenomena seem to hide mysterious messages – is a projection of Wozzeck's own mind and, since this is the only world that the opera presents to us, we are forced to share Wozzeck's experiences and to identify with him. Despite the work's innovative features, however, the aesthetics of *Wozzeck* are those of nineteenth-century operas and of the Wagnerian music drama. Berg's own remarks on *Wozzeck* in his 1928 article on 'The Problem of Opera', in which he declared that his intentions when writing the piece were 'nothing else than to render to the theatre what is the theatre's, and that means to shape the music in such a way that it is aware at every moment of its duty to serve the drama',[7] reveal, in unmistakable terms, his allegiance to the Wagnerian aesthetic. When Erich Kleiber mounted a new production of *Wozzeck* at the Berlin Staatsoper in November 1932, Max Marschalk, the critic of the *Vossische Zeitung* wrote:

From this distance we can see that the new opera has two main paths. One path goes from Wagner through Strauss to Berg, where it seems for the moment to have ended. The other, going from Mussorgsky and Debussy to Janáček and Stravinsky and then on to Milhaud and Kurt Weill, is the really modern and new path. The essential difference becomes clear at two points. Berg holds aloof from the modern epic theatre – although Büchner's *Woyzeck* with its loosely ordered succession of short scenes and the cold objective attitude of the poet towards his characters stands close to the repressed emotions of epic theatre. Through his music, however, Berg turns the whole of the drama into something emotional . . . just as earlier operas did. Stravinsky and Weill write music against the words; Berg composes wholly from within the words drawing from their emotional content a psychological, poetising music . . .[8]

Weill himself saw *Wozzeck* in a similar light. Reviewing the Berlin première of the opera in 1925, Weill called *Wozzeck* 'a masterpiece of the strongest power' and described the performance as 'the greatest event in Berlin's musical life for many years'[9] but regarded the work as 'the grandiose conclusion' of traditional

Wagnerian music drama.[10] Despite the antipathy of Schoenberg and Webern both to the music of Weill and to the idea of the 'new opera' (an idea which Schoenberg himself parodied in *Von Heute auf Morgen*), the dramatic method of *Lulu* has much in common with that of Weill and Brecht's 'epic opera'. As a man of the theatre Berg could not afford to ignore, and could not fail to be interested in, what was happening in the 'new opera'. Like Schoenberg, Berg probably knew Brecht's and Weill's writing on the epic theatre and, perhaps, on *Mahagonny*. He certainly knew *Mahagonny* itself and attended rehearsals of the opera when it was being performed in Vienna in 1932, when it was conducted by his own pupil Gottfried Kassowitz and directed by Hans Heinsheimer of Universal Edition, Berg's own publishers.

Writing about *The Threepenny Opera* Brecht says:

> The tenderest and most moving love-song in the play described the eternal, indestructable mutual attachment of a procurer and his girl ... In such a way the music, just because it took up a purely emotional attitude and spurned none of the stock narcotic attractions, became an active collaborator in the stripping bare of the middle class corpus of ideas.[11]

Time after time in *Lulu* we become conscious of the disturbing difference between the emotional attitude adopted by the music and the nature of the text to which it is set. It is difficult when reading Brecht's description of the love duet in the *Threepenny Opera* not to think of the love duet and *Hymn* at the end of Act II of *Lulu* when the listener is most forcibly made aware of the distinction between the luxuriousness and overwhelming emotional intensity of the music, the unpleasantness of the dramatic situation (as Alwa declares his love for the woman who was his step-mother, step-sister and the murderess of his father) and the absurdity of the text in which Alwa, the composer, compares parts of Lulu's anatomy to musical terms.

Many commentators on *Lulu* have been disturbed by, and have been unable to account for, this aspect of the opera. Over thirty years ago, Donald Mitchell suggested that Berg had unconsciously precipitated a large-scale dramatic confusion because, said Mitchell, 'what goes on in the orchestra pit and on the stage fail to match'.[12] Reviewing the Paris première of the complete *Lulu*, the composer Robin Holloway remarked that the dislocation of 'one's sense of relationship between music and character' was such that 'if one is concentrating on action and character the music seems completely inappropriate'.[13] Sir Colin Davis's remarks, quoted in chapter 3, on his own experience when directing the work at the Royal Opera House ('sometimes I feel that there is almost no connection between what's happening on the stage and what I am doing in the orchestra pit') were intended as an observation on this pecularity of the work itself, not as a comment on the Covent Garden production.[14]

This division between music and action in *Lulu* cannot be accounted for if we consider the opera only in relation to *Wozzeck* and to the works of the Second Viennese School. If, however, we consider *Lulu* in relation to what was happening at the same time in the 'new opera' – if, for example, we think of the way in which the music and text work against one another in a piece such as *Mahagonny* or think of the 'cold objectivity' that Marschalk cites as one of the characteristics of the epic theatre of the period – then what Berg is attempting in *Lulu* becomes clearer. Indeed, Robin Holloway comes close to seeing this as the solution when, in the review quoted above, he observes that *Lulu* 'contradicts its own intensity and undermines its listeners' obedience to emotive instructions' in what amounts to 'a reversal of the expressionist aesthetic'.[15]

With their lack of traditional characterization and their fragmentary structure, Wedekind's *Lulu* plays already fulfil two of the requirements of epic theatre. Transferred from the theatre to the opera house, the absurdities of Wedekind's tortuous plot become what Brecht described *Mahagonny* to be – a conscious tribute to the irrationality of operatic form. 'One could write an interesting opera about this', says Alwa (who, as the music tells us, is Berg himself) in the third scene of Act I. Although he rejects the idea, saying that such an opera would be too absurd, Alwa's opera does get written – it is the opera that we are watching – but it has a plot that even the characters involved find difficult to believe. Time and again the work turns back on itself, questioning its own basis (as, for example, it does in Act II, scene 2, when the Athlete accuses Alwa of having written an opera that no decent theatre will stage) and reminding us, as epic theatre requires, that what we are seeing is not reality but merely an artistic artefact. It warns us, that is, not to confuse art with reality – a warning that goes unheeded by Alwa, for one, who, ineffectual and concerned only with his own artistic pretensions, confuses art and reality to such an extent that he manages to get himself killed in his own opera. It is a particularly telling indictment since, as we have seen, Alwa has been specifically identified as Berg himself – Berg who, as recent research has revealed, was perhaps more prone to confuse art and life than any other composer.[16]

If Brecht and Weill require that the audience, recognizing that what is on the stage is not 'real life', adopts an objective un-emotional attitude which will allow it to make a moral judgment about what is being presented, Berg equally ensures that, until the very end of the opera, the audience is not able to identify or become emotionally involved with the characters of his opera.

But *Lulu* contravenes Brecht's ideas of how epic theatre should work in at least two respects – and it is these two un-Brechtian aspects that make *Lulu* so powerful, so moral and so disturbing a work. In the famous table showing those changes of emphasis which distinguish 'epic' from 'dramatic' theatre,[17] Brecht opposes 'involvement' and 'observation', remarking that whereas the dramatic theatre provides the spectator with sensation by implicating and involving him in the stage action, the epic theatre, by contrast, turns the spectator into an observer, it makes him face up to an argument and forces him to take decisions about what he is seeing presented on the stage.

Feeling, it is suggested, makes such decisions impossible. The chief aims of traditional opera, argues Brecht, are illusion and sensual satisfaction; it encourages the listener to become emotionally involved and to identify with the characters on stage – to become, as he puts it, 'wax in the magician's hands' – and in this it precludes the listener from making moral judgments. In opera 'all discussion of content is excluded' says Brecht, because 'if a member of the audience had to take up a position in relation to a particular set of circumstances portrayed, the spell would have been broken and opera would have lost its battle'.[18] *Lulu*, however, not only disproves, but turns on its head, the thesis that emotional involvement precludes moral decision. Brecht regarded a certain kind of music as being a prerequisite for the creation of epic theatre, and the musical language of *Lulu* is of a kind that he would undoubtedly have regarded as being unacceptably élitist, esoteric and sensual – the sort of music that, in his essay 'On the Use of Music in an Epic Theatre', he described as 'complicated music of a mainly psychological kind'. Yet it is precisely the sensual, emotional power of Berg's music that forces us to face up to the moral argument of *Lulu*.

Although the fact that what we are seeing on stage has something to do with us in the audience is pointed out throughout the opera it is only in the final scene that the relevance of these events is brought home not just intellectually but, more tellingly, emotionally as well. Until this point Berg has deliberately prevented us from becoming emotionally involved in the stage action. Now, in the final scene, and in particular in the passage analysed in the previous chapter, Berg reverses this strategy. We are finally compelled, through the intensity and power of the music, to feel pity for and to identify not only with Lulu and Geschwitz, whose sexually 'abnormal' but self-sacrificing love is presented as a positive alternative to the brutal, uncomprehending and possessive sexuality of the male figures, but with all the characters helplessly trapped in this grotesque *Totentanz*. It is through that act of identification that we are made to face our moral responsibility for the society depicted on stage.

This is a supremely un-Brechtian device and one that cuts across the distinctions between 'epic' and 'dramatic' theatre, for it is through involving us in the stage action (something that Brecht regarded as being characteristic of 'dramatic' theatre) that Berg brings us to that point of moral recognition that is the aim of epic theatre.

Brecht also believed that it was impossible to make the spectator face up to an argument and face a moral decision within the confines of the traditional operatic conventions. The apparatus of commercial opera would, he argued, inevitably control those attempting to employ it. The new 'epic opera' could only be created if one first dismantled the paraphernalia of traditional opera.

Here again, *Lulu* questions – if not contradicts – these assumptions. *Lulu*, more effectively and more dangerously, attacks the form from within by both employing and at the same time containing within itself a criticism of the conventions of traditional opera. *Lulu* is an opera about writing an opera; consequently, whereas the structure of *Wozzeck* is based on the formal designs of abstract instrumental music that of *Lulu* uses those vocal forms – arias, recitatives, cavatinas and so on – that are traditionally associated with opera. And *Lulu* not only pays its respects to the conventions of opera – by referring, as George Perle has pointed out, to the traditional 'ensemble of perplexity' in the *Canon* of Act II, scene 1, for example[19] – but even to specific works within the operatic tradition; to *Tristan und Isolde*, for example, in its final *Liebestod* for the Countess Geschwitz and in its quotation of the

Tristan chord as the accompaniment to Alwa's declaration of love in Act II.

But its being couched in the conventions of traditional opera are a vital part of *Lulu*'s subversive tactics, and it exploits not only the musical but also the social conventions of opera. In equating us who watch the opera with the stage audience at the cabaret it exploits the conventional relationship between stage and auditorium; it exploits what George Steiner has called 'the convention of people in fancy dress in the audience watching people in fancy dress on stage pouring out great lyric sentiments, grave subjects, the tension never completely resolved between a realistic stage setting on the one hand and, on the other, the completely stylised formal techniques'.[20] Above all it exploits the fact that the audience for opera, far more than the audience for the spoken theatre, is conservative, bourgeois and goes to the opera house expecting what Brecht called 'an evening's entertainment'. Berg's *Lulu* in the opera house is far more shocking than are the Wedekind plays in the theatre simply because of the nature of opera and the nature of opera audiences. We can accept the cynical, satirical treatment of low-life in the 'new opera' of *Mahagonny* and *The Threepenny Opera* but we do not (despite the precedent of *La Traviata*) expect traditional opera to deal with the kind of subjects *Lulu* deals with. The very choice of the Wedekind *Lulu* plays is, therefore, a deliberate act of subversion and provocation. And this, of course, is part of Berg's plan because it is the hypocrisy of the society represented by the opera's own audience that is the subject of the work. Rather than the apparatus controlling the operatic product, as Brecht claimed, in *Lulu* the operatic product uses and subverts the apparatus for its own ends. *Lulu* is a Trojan horse, smuggled into the very heart of the enemy camp.

At the centre of the two plays stands the figure of Lulu herself, a figure without an ancestry ('I never had a mother' she says in Act II, scene 1 of the opera), whom Wedekind invests with a variety of mythical and elemental associations (Earth spirit, Pandora, Eve) while leaving their precise symbolic significance ambiguous. Some writers have seen Lulu as an embodiment of 'the *femme fatale*, the *belle dame sans merci*, the man-eating, man-devouring vamp – part of that awesome and haunting stock which fills Western poetry and art and literature'.[21] But Lulu is presented as neither a man-eater nor an avenging fury; her role, as Wedekind himself emphasized in his defence of *Pandora's Box*, is entirely passive. We know from the memoirs of his wife Tilly Wedekind (the first stage-Lulu) that Wedekind himself wanted the role played 'like a Madonna, rather than as a wild animal who had already devoured a couple of men for breakfast. "It is no longer possible to take the play seriously if the part is played like that", Wedekind used to say.'[22] The character of Lulu, like the symbolism of her mythic associations and the meaning of the plays themselves, remains ambiguous and open to different interpretations. Elizabeth Boa, in her book on Wedekind,[23] has given numerous examples of the diverse and conflicting critical interpretations to which the *Lulu* plays have given rise, with different critics seeing the plays as supporting their own, often radically opposed, beliefs. To some critics Lulu is a typical bourgeois male fantasy, to others the scourge of the bourgeoisie; to some she represents the female sexual drive at the centre of life, to others the elemental principle of destruction; to some the plays are an affirmation of the need for social order, to others an affirmation of the liberating need for pleasure.

Such diverse reactions, however, spring from the critics' response to Wedekind's texts. The structure and the emotional intensity of Berg's music imposes its own interpretation on these texts, an interpretation which, if we respond to the music and approach the opera on Berg's, rather than Wedekind's, terms, confronts us with a stark choice.

Unlike *Wozzeck*, *Lulu* allows us no easy emotional release. The great D minor interlude in *Wozzeck*, played by the orchestra alone with the curtain down, acts as an emotional catharsis in which the listener responds directly to the power of the music. The end of *Lulu* is more ambiguous. The music of the final pages of the opera has an emotional intensity not unlike that of the *Wozzeck* interlude, but its effect is very different. The music that comes back at this point of the opera is music that brings with it a host of complex and conflicting associations, some of which have been touched on in the previous chapter. The return of Schön's Sonata Coda theme is played, not with the curtain down but as an accompaniment to the sordid transaction between Lulu and Jack; the final appearance of Lulu's entrance music is heard as she leaves the stage for the last time and the closing Adagio is a *Liebestod* sung by the dying Countess Geschwitz. The difference between the luxuriant, elegiac music and the events on stage produces an emotional disorientation that is deeply disturbing; it can also, if we respond to the music and are prepared to give these characters the understanding and compassion that the humanity of Berg's score demands, be humanly restorative. Whether or not we regard Jack as a creature from the dark depths of our own subconscious, *Lulu* forces us to face a part of ourselves that we would rather not acknowledge. Despite, or perhaps because of, its absurdities *Lulu* touches not on the unreal but on something that is too real and too close to us for us to feel comfortable or complacent about the work. In the end we must either reject the piece outright or we must face those aspects of ourselves to which we would rather not admit but which this extraordinary opera forces us to confront.

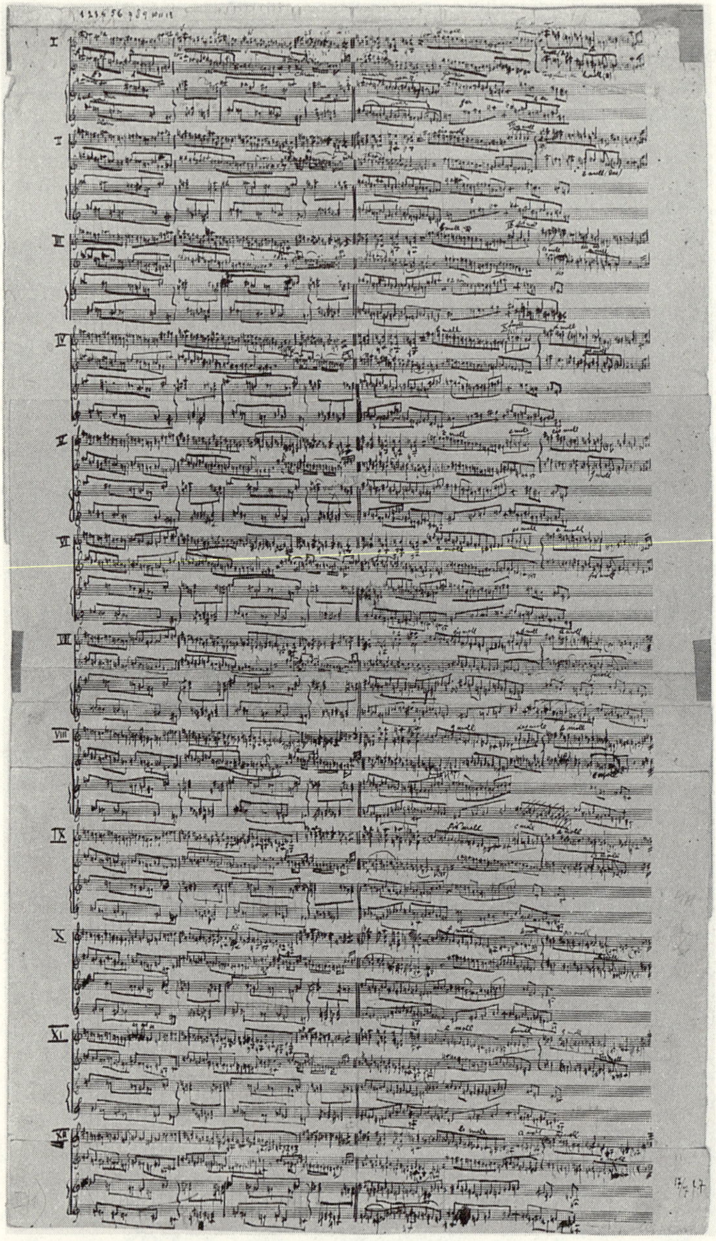

Plate 1a/1b Berg's 1927 row chart for the Basic Set of *Lulu* and some of its derivative rows

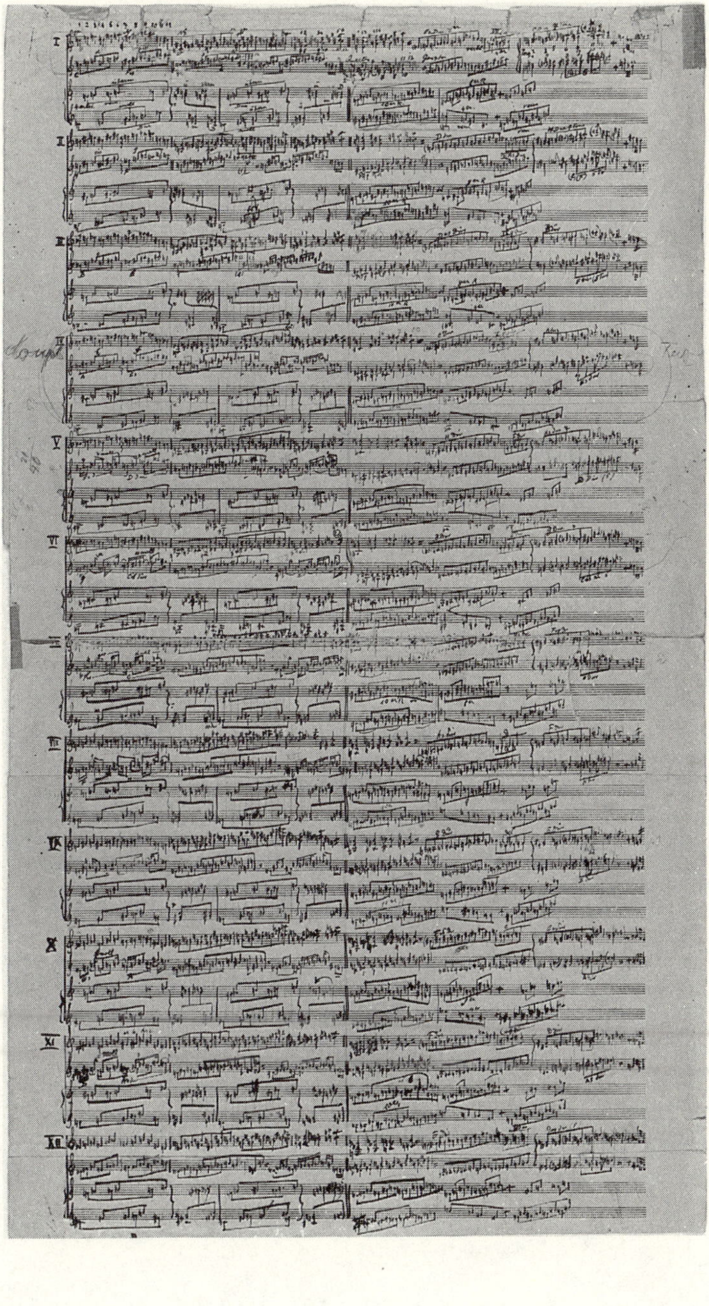

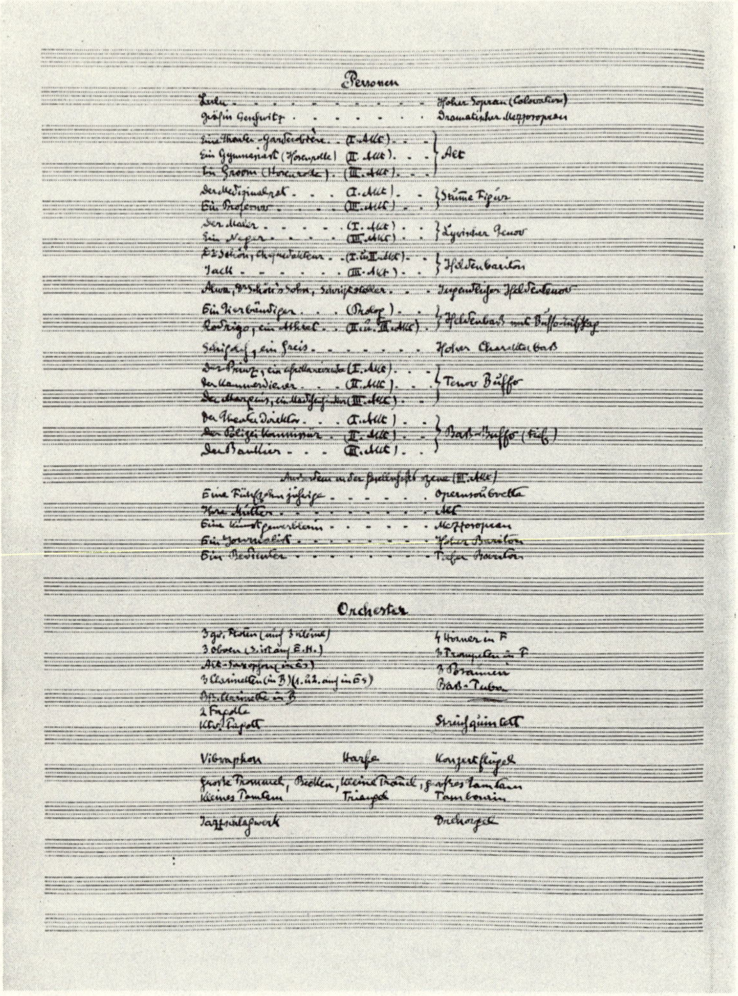

Plate 2 The handwritten dramatis personae from the fair copy of the prologue to *Lulu* which Berg sent as a sixtieth-birthday present to Schoenberg in September 1934

Plate 3   Zurich 1937. The world première of *Lulu*. Act I, scene 3.
Asger Stig (Dr Schön). Directed by Karl Schmid-Blos; sets by Roman
Clemens; costumes by Jörg Stockar

Plate 4   Paris Opera 1979. The world première of the complete three-act *Lulu*. The death of Dr Schön, with Act II 'converted into an evening party in the 1920s'. Teresa Stratas (Lulu), Franz Mazura (Dr Schön). Directed by Patrice Chereau; sets by Richard Peduzzi; costumes by Jacques Schmidt

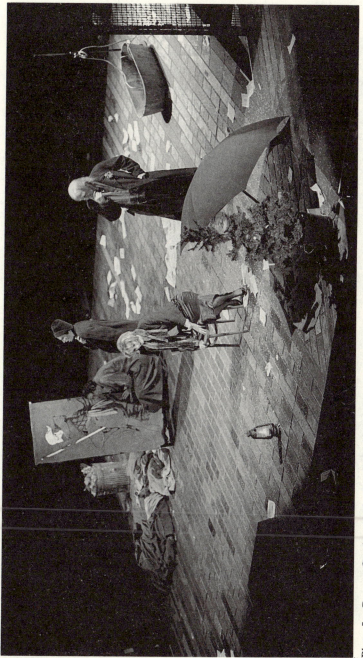

Plate 5   Covent Garden 1983. The British première of the complete three-act *Lulu*. Act III, scene 2, the London attic converted into 'the roof garden at Derry and Thom's'. Karen Armstrong (Lulu), Erik Saeden (Schigolch), Brigitte Fassbaender (Countess Geschwitz). Directed by Götz Friedrich; designed by Timothy O'Brien

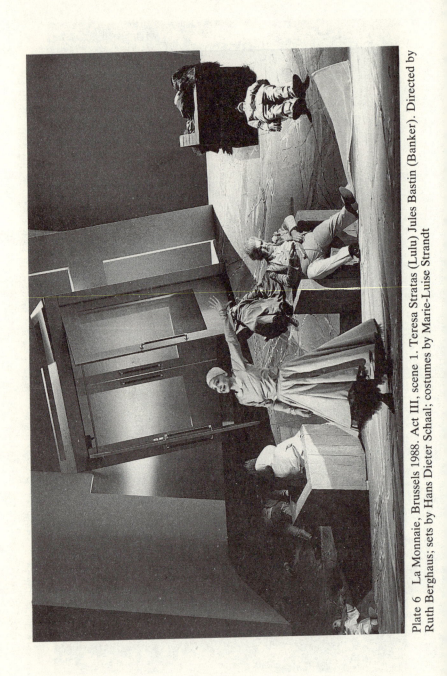

Plate 6 La Monnaie, Brussels 1988. Act III, scene 1. Teresa Stratas (Lulu) Jules Bastin (Banker). Directed by Ruth Berghaus; sets by Hans Dieter Schaal; costumes by Marie-Luise Strandt

Plate 7   Scottish Opera, Glasgow 1987. Act II, scene 1. The death of Dr Schön. Beverly Morgan (Lulu), Chester Ludgin (Dr Schön). Directed by John Cox; sets by John Bury; costumes by Elizabeth Bury

Document 1:   *Pandora's Box*

KARL KRAUS

... The love of women holds within it, like Pandora's box, all
life's ills, but they are enclosed in golden petals and are so full of
colours and scents that it is impossible to regret having opened
the box. The scents ward off old age and retain their innate
strength to the end. Every moment of happiness has its own price,
and I die a little from the effect of these sweet, subtle scents rising
from that evil box; yet my hand, though already tremulous with
age, still finds strength to turn forbidden keys. What are life,
fame, art? I would give them all for those blissful hours on
summer nights when my head lay pillowed on breasts shaped like
the goblet of the King of Thule – now, like it, vanished and
gone...
                                                        Félicien Rops

'A soul rubbing the sleep out of its eyes in the next world.' A poet
and lover, hesitating between love and the artistic projection of
female beauty, holds Lulu's hand in his and speaks the words which
are the key to this maze of femininity, the labyrinth in which many a
man has lost the thread of his reason. It is the last act of *Erdgeist*
(*Earth Spirit*). The queen of love has gathered around her all types
of manhood so that they may serve her and take what she has to
give. Alwa, the son of her husband, says as much. And then, when
he has drunk his fill at this sweet fount of perdition, when his
destiny has fulfilled itself, in the last act of *Pandora's Box*, he will,
delirious in the contemplation of Lulu's portrait, formulate these
words:

Looking at this portrait I find my self-respect again. It makes my fate
comprehensible to me. Everything we have experienced becomes so
natural, so inevitable, so crystal clear. He who still feels secure in his
bourgeois attitudes when confronted with these full, rounded lips, these
great, innocent, childlike eyes, this pink and white, healthy body, let him
cast the first stone at us.

These words are spoken as he gazes at the portrait of the woman
who became the destroyer of everyone, because she was destroyed

102

by everyone, and they encompass the world of the author, Frank
Wedekind. A world in which woman, if she matures towards
aesthetic perfection, is not condemned to take from man the cross
of moral responsibility. An intuition which can comprehend the
tragic gulf between full, rounded lips and bourgeois attitudes may
perhaps be the only one today worthy of a dramatist. The factual
foundations of *Pandora's Box* are laid in *Earth Spirit*, but the
intellectual content of the whole work is only made comprehensible
by the second play; anyone who has understood the *Lulu* tragedy
will have the same emotional reaction to the whole of German
literature that the grown-up would have when faced with being
taught his two-times table, for it is a literature which fastens on
woman like a parasite and takes psychological advantage of the
'relationship between the sexes'. I would not hesitate to open this
vast parade of childish psychological nonsense with many a classical
author. The most profound explorers of the emotional life of the
male begin to stammer when their heroines turn their gaze on
them, and the unspeakable tragedy to which they give expression
has always been the tragedy of lost virginity. Throughout the
history of our drama, right up to our own day, we hear some old
fogy muttering 'Don't you dare go on the streets', or even simply,
furtively, 'Don't you dare. . .': time and again we see the plot of a
drama turning on the loss of a maidenhead. Never in such cases
have writers seen themselves as saviours of humanity; they feel
bowed, like their fellow humans, under the sword of Damocles
which humanity in Christian humility has hung over itself of its own
accord. Gullibly they have revered the mistaken notion that the
world's honour is diminished when its joy increases. And they have
written tragedies on the subject of 'what no man can escape from'.
The fact that it is far less easy to avoid the rough and ready
platitudes of a philosophical carpenter than the unfortunate escapades of his Mary Magdalene is a literary fact in its own right.[2] But
Frank Wedekind was the first to turn his back on all this theatrical
moaning and groaning about the devaluing of the market value of
nubile young women. In his play *Hidalla*, which is in part a personal
confession, Fanny manages to rise high above the suitor who has
turned her down because she lacked the 'advantage' which alone
makes young women a good proposition: 'So that's why I am
nothing any more! So that was my main attraction! Is it possible to
think up a more despicable criticism of any human being – than to
be loved for the sake of an "advantage" like that – as if one were

cattle!...' And then we have the powerful double tragedy, the second part of which you will see today, the eternal tragedy of misunderstood and persecuted feminine charm which a despicable world allows only to climb into the Procrustean bed of its own moral principles. The play depicts a woman running the gauntlet: a woman not intended by her Creator to serve the egotism of her possessor, who can only rise to achieve her true worth if allowed her freedom. The fleeting beauty of a tropical bird gives greater happiness than its permanent possession, when a cramped cage has spoiled its lovely plumage: but this is something no bird-catcher has yet admitted. A man may dream about having a free female companion; but reality will force her to belong to him as wife or mistress, because his need for social respectability will always take precedence over his dreams. Thus even the man who wishes to have a polyandrous wife wants her for himself. This simple desire must be regarded as the basis of all love tragedies: the man's desire to be chosen without allowing the woman the right to choose. No Oberon is ever willing to understand that even his own Titania can be enamoured of an ass, because his greater powers of reflection and lesser sexual readiness would make him incapable of any similar infatuation. Thus men in love make asses of themselves. Without a full measure of social esteem they cannot survive: and this can lead them to become thieves and murderers! And the ghostly spectre of love slips away between the corpses – love in which a world constricted by social *idées fixes* has allowed all the attractive features of woman to become vices.

It is one of these dramatic conflicts between feminine nature and a male blockhead that has delivered Lulu into the hands of temporal justice, and she would have nine years in prison to reflect on the fact that beauty is a punishment sent from God, if her devoted love-slaves did not concoct a plan for her release. The plan is a romantic one, which in the real world could not ripen even in the most fanciful of brains, or be made to succeed even by the most fanatical of wills. But it is with the freeing of Lulu that *Pandora's Box* begins; and with the success of this impossible venture the author illustrates the readiness of the love-enslaved to sacrifice themselves, and does it more effectively than if he had chosen a more plausible motif. In *Earth Spirit* it was Lulu who carried the action; in *Pandora's Box* she is carried by it. It is more clearly evident here than earlier on that the tragic heroine of the drama is in fact her beauty: her portrait, the picture of her painted when at the height of her beauty, plays a more important role than Lulu herself. Earlier her charms were what moved the action on, whereas now the audience watches her moving along a *via dolorosa* where at every turn its emotions are aroused by the contrast between her former glory and her present wretched state. The great reprisal has begun, a men's world is brashly taking revenge for its own guilt. 'This woman', says Alwa, 'shot my father in this room, yet I cannot see the murder and the punishment as other than a terrible misfortune which has befallen her. I also believe that if my father had come out of it alive he would not have withdrawn his support from her completely.' Alwa, Schön's surviving son, here displays a sensitivity and sympathy which he has in common with the boy Alfred Hugenberg, whose touching infatuation ends in suicide. But a quite exceptionally absorbing and touching alliance is formed by Alwa and Lulu's friend Countess Geschwitz, who has great strength of character and is ready and happy to sacrifice herself. It is a heterosexual alliance which, however, allows both of them to succumb to the spell of Lulu, who is sex personified. They are the true prisoners of their own love for her. They seem to lap up every disappointment and every hurt that come from a loved one incapable of non-physical gratitude, and they go on affirming her good points even at the brink of each new abyss. Their way of thinking is, broadly speaking, that of Wedekind, however much theirs diverges from his in specific details. Something of it is expressed in a Shakespeare sonnet written centuries earlier:

> How sweet and lovely dost thou make the shame
> Which, like a canker in the fragrant rose
> Doth spot the beauty of thy budding name!
> O! in what sweets dost thou thy sins enclose.
> That tongue that tells the story of thy days,
> Making lascivious comments on thy sport,
> Cannot dispraise but in a kind of praise;
> Naming thy name blesses an ill report.
> O! what a mansion have those vices got
> Which for their habitation chose out thee,
> Where beauty's veil doth cover every blot
> And all things turn to fair that eyes can see![3]

It can also be called – to use the silly medical word derived from a novelist's name – masochism. Perhaps this is the basis of artistic sensibility. The 'possession' of the woman, the man's security in being 'beatus possidens', is something that cannot bring happiness except to someone lacking in imagination. This is the *Realpolitik* of love. Rodrigo Quast, the athlete, has got himself a hippopotamus whip with which he will make her not only 'the most impressive trapeze artiste of the future, already here today', but also a faithful wife who will be allowed to receive only admirers of whom he personally approves. This incomparable philosopher, this man who depends on prostitutes' earnings, is the first in the line of Lulu's tormentors: from now on men will all recompense her with meanness for the sins they commit against her through stupidity. The succession of those who, loving her, want her for themselves is ineluctably followed by the succession of those who just want sex: first in this procession comes Rodrigo, who has unfortunately forgotten how to 'balance two saddled cavalry horses on his rib-cage', and then Casti-Piani, whose villainous face has gained a different, more evil sadistic power over Lulu's sexual will. In order to escape from one blackmailer she has to throw herself into the arms of the next, becoming everyone's victim and sacrificing each one, until, exhausted, she encounters the ultimate and quintessential avenger of the male sex – Jack the Ripper. From Hugenberg, the most sensitive, her path leads her to Jack, the most sexual, and she is drawn to him like a moth to a flame. He is the most sadistic of all her tormentors, and his knife becomes a symbol: it takes from her the means by which she sinned against them all.

For the attentive observer, a loose chain of events such as might have been dreamt up by a writer of cheap fiction builds up into a world of glimpsed possibilities, of moods and shocks, and the gutter poetry becomes the true poetry of the gutter, which can be condemned only by that feeble-minded, conventional outlook which prefers a badly painted palace to a beautifully painted hovel. But the truth lies behind scenes like these rather than in them. In Wedekind's world people live for the sake of ideas; there would be little room in it for the realistic depiction of living conditions. Wedekind is the first German dramatist to reintroduce thought to a stage from which it had long been absent. All the trappings of naturalistic depiction have vanished. What occupies people and makes them tick is more important than what dialect they speak.[4] They even have monologues – a word one dare hardly whisper – and they have them even when others are on stage with them. The curtain rises to reveal an overweight athlete day-dreaming of fat wages and earnings from prostitutes, a poet fulminating like Karl Moor[5] against living in an age of clerks and pen-pushers, and a suffering woman dreaming of being rescued by the female friend

whom she worships – three characters who speak but whose words
pass the others by. They are of three different worlds. It is a
dramatic technique rather like juggling with three balls. It gives one
an inkling that there is a higher form of naturalism than that
conveyed by the trivial realities so laboriously paraded before our
eyes by the German literature of the last twenty years. Wedekind's
language represents an amazing blend of accurate characterization
and heightened aphorism. Every word, whether in speech patterns
or catch-phrases, is perfectly suited both to the character and to his
or her thoughts and destiny. The pimp says: 'Women are of a
practical turn of mind, so feeding their men isn't half the trouble to
them that it would be the other way round. Provided that the men
do all the thinking for them and don't let their sense of family go by
the board.' How would one of our so-called realists have expressed
this? Scenes such as that between Alwa and Lulu in Act I, between
Casti-Piani and Lulu in Act II, and above all the one in the last act
in which Geschwitz bursts into the London squalor with Lulu's
portrait – no other German dramatist, even with the most highly
polished technique for creating atmosphere, could have brought
these off, and no other writer would have had the courage or the
power to probe so deep into the human heart. There is a Shake-
spearean grotesque quality, equalled only by real life, in the
alternation between burlesque and tragic effects, seen at its most
extreme where a character is convulsed with emotion while pulling
on boots. It is like a street-ballad with visionary overtones, a
melodrama on the deeper significance of the theme of 'step by step
down the slippery slope'; outwardly it seems like a picture drawn
from life, but seen from inside, it is a symbol of life itself. Events
succeed each other as in a delirious dream, dreamed by an author
made ill by his own creation, Lulu. At the end Alwa might pass his
hand over his eyes and awake in the arms of a woman who is just
rubbing the sleep from her eyes in the next world. This second act,
the one which takes place in Paris, has the dull colouring of a
shabby life of pleasure: everything is as if seen through a gauze; it is
no more than a stage in the parallel calvaries of Lulu and Alwa. She
front-stage, crumpling up a note from a blackmailer; he behind in
the gaming-room with a forged share certificate in his hand. Drunk
with degradation, he hurries on towards the abyss. A confused
blur of gamblers and women of easy virtue, all being tricked by
a dishonest banker. Everything very schematic and couched in a
language that consciously keeps to the conventional tones of a

dialogue in a novelette: 'Well, my friend, come on; let's go and try our hand at baccarat.' The 'Marquis' Casti-Piani appears on stage not in the minor character role of a white slave trader but as the incarnation of the white slave trade. A mere couple of sentences throw a harsh social floodlight only subdued by the curtain; the ironic content is so strong that it renders superfluous a hundred pamphlets criticizing our mendacious society and our hypocritical state. A character who is both a police spy and a pimp says:

The public prosecutor will pay a thousand marks to anyone who can deliver into his hands the murderess of Dr Schön. I need only to whistle to the policeman standing down there at the corner to earn a thousand marks. On the other hand the establishment of Oikonomopoulos in Cairo is offering sixty pounds for you. That's twelve hundred marks – two hundred more than the public prosecutor is offering.

And when Lulu tries to buy him off with shareholdings: 'I've never bothered with shares. The public prosecutor pays in the currency of the German Reich and Oikonomopoulos pays in English gold.' The man most immediately responsible for upholding public morality and the representative of the firm of Oikonomopoulos are one and the same. A ghostly flitting and hustling, a degree of dramatic allusion which Offenbach captured in his settings of E. T. A. Hoffmann, such as the Olympia act. Like Spalanzani, the adoptive father of an automaton, this man Puntschu cheats society with his forged share certificates. In a few sentences spoken in monologue, his diabolical mischievousness finds a philosophical expression that sums up the differences between the sexes more profoundly than all the wisdom of the medical specialists. He emerges from the gaming room chuckling impishly over the fact that his Jewish morality is that much more acceptable than the morals of the women clustering around him. They have to hire out their sex, their 'Josaphat', whereas he can help himself by his native wit. Poor girls, they have to pay out their only capital, their bodies, whereas the quick-wittedness of the rogue preserves him intact, 'and he doesn't need to bathe in eau de Cologne!' Thus the immorality of the man triumphs over the amorality of the woman. In Act III, cosh, revolver and butcher's knife make their appearance; and it is out of these dismal manifestations of a hard factual world that the purest notes ring out. The unspeakable things that happen at this point will repel anyone who asks of art only that it should provide relaxation, or thinks that it should never overstep the bounds of his own capacity to suffer; but the judgment of such a person would be just as weak as his nerves if he were to deny the superlative quality of this dramatic achievement. Of course, if one expects realism one will not wish to enter into this feverish experience in a London garret any more than one will go along with the 'unrealistic' liberation of Lulu in Act I or the elimination of Rodrigo in Act II. And when Lulu has finally become a prostitute and is seen receiving four clients one after another, some spectators may receive a crude titillation, but in this alternation of grotesque and tragic impressions and this succession of horrible faces there is a poetic inspiration which they fail to see. Such people have no right to complain that their ability to be receptive and sensitive has been underestimated. It serves them right to be living in the age of the dramatic movement so bitterly criticized by Frank Wedekind through the mouth of his character Alwa. But surely no one could possibly be so myopic as to be misled by the uncomfortableness of the dramatic content into failing to recognise the brilliance of the dramatist's treatment of it and the inherent necessity of his choice; the cosh, revolver and knife surely cannot prevent one from seeing that this sex murder is accomplished like a destiny whose origins lie in the furthest depths of the female nature; and surely no one should be misled by the Countess Geschwitz's lesbianism into forgetting that she has greatness and that, far from representing an average pathological case, she strides through the tragedy like a demonic negation of joy. Of course, the infinite subtleties of this apparently coarse piece of writing only reveal themselves to the reader on closer study: Lulu's premonition of her end, which throws its shadow even over the first act, her preordained enthralment, and her serene unawareness of the fates of the men who have fallen victim to her. When she hears the news of young Hugenberg's death in prison, she asks 'if he is in prison too', and the only effect of Alwa's corpse on her is to make the room less cosy. Then the instant recognition of Jack, who strokes the head of that most unfeminine of women, Geschwitz, like that of a dog and immediately takes stock of her relationship with Lulu and thus pityingly realizes her unsuitability for his dreadful need. 'This monster is quite safe from me', he says of Geschwitz after stabbing her to death. He does not murder her in pursuit of sex, but simply in order to get rid of an obstacle. The only way he could get satisfaction from her would be to cut out her brain.

It cannot be too strongly emphasized how dangerous it is to seek the essence of this piece of writing in its unusual subject-matter.

One school of criticism, whose homely, healthy approach does not bother itself over-much about affairs of the heart, has chosen to dismiss *Earth Spirit* as nothing more than a piece of *grand guignol* in which the author has mixed horror with smut. A leading Berlin intellectual has revealed his cluelessness regarding the world of this two-part play by advising its gifted author to hurry up and choose more suitable material. As if the author could 'choose' his material like a tailor, or like a journalist in a Sunday paper, who can take other people's opinions and clothe them in his own style. Contemporary German critics have absolutely no idea of the primeval forces which here generated the subject-matter and the form simultaneously. We have all come to accept certain things without question: the fact that the legitimate stage imagines its ideal of modernity to be fulfilled in its annual quota of well-made plays, the fact that the blessing of royalties constantly rewards the mediocre, and that the only distinction that a truly creative personality enjoys is that it receives no Schiller prize, Grillparzer prize, or whatever the reward for hard work, sound morals and lack of talent may be called. But it is indeed bitterly ironic that a playwright whose every line contains a perfect blend of thought and technical know-how is treated as a freak by the artistic establishment, even though his trains of thought open up illuminating vistas that point beyond the pathetic contemporary concern with heredity and environment. Such a dramatist is seen as 'grotesque'. And with this verdict the self-righteous – who in literary matters always kill two birds with one slogan – think they have written him off. As if to be grotesque were always an end in itself to serve the whim of the artist! His critics mistake the mask for the face, and none has the least idea that the cover of grotesqueness may be identical with an idealist's sense of decency – the idealist who remains an idealist even when he confesses in one of his poems that he would rather be a whore than the 'happiest and most famous of men', and whose sense of decency reaches into spheres far deeper than that of those people whose sensibilities are offended by certain material.

The reproach that a writer has 'put something into' a literary work is surely the highest praise. For those shallow dramas whose ceiling is hardly separated from their floor are those into which, with the best will in the world, it would be impossible to 'put' anything. On the other hand, the true masterpiece, in which the author has created his own world, is one into which anyone can put or read anything. Make no mistake about it, the events in *Pando-*

ra's Box can be included in our discussion of woman from a moral as well as an aesthetic standpoint. The question whether the playwright is more concerned with depicting her in her happy heyday than with the exploring of her disastrous influence is one which each individual can answer as he thinks fit. Thus even the judge of public morals has his money's worth, for he sees the appalling consequences of immorality portrayed with exemplary clarity; for him the emphasis will be more on Jack's bloodstained knife as the instrument of a liberating act than on Lulu as the tragic victim. So an audience which does not like the subject-matter has no cause to get worked up about its sentiments and intentions. This is a pity, as I for one find these quite bad enough. In Lulu we see the depiction of a woman whom men think they are 'having' while in fact they are being 'had' by her, a woman who is something different for each of them, who shows each a different face and is more seldom unfaithful, more virginal, than the average domestic doll. In her I see the perfect vindication of immorality, in the depiction of a complete woman who has the inspired ability not to be able to remember, a woman who lives without inhibitions but also without the dangers of constant mental conception, and who swills away every experience into oblivion. She is ruled by desire, but not the desire to give birth; she wants to give pleasure, not to preserve the race. Hers is not the broken lock of womanhood; hers is constantly open and constantly closed again. She is detached from any desire to give life, but is herself born again with each new act of love. A sleepwalker of love who only 'falls' when her name is called; eternally the giver and the loser. The philosophical rogue says of her in the drama: 'She cannot live by love, because her life is love.' Yet in this narrow-minded world the source of pleasure inevitably becomes a Pandora's box; and it seems to me that the whole work springs from this infinitely regrettable fact.

The next campaign of liberation for humanity

writes Wedekind in his more programmatic work *Hidalla*

will be directed against the feudalism of love. The shame which people feel regarding their own feelings belongs to the age of alchemy and witch-hunts. Isn't there something ludicrous about a human race that keeps secrets from itself? Or do you perhaps believe in the vulgar notion that one's love-life must be hidden because it is something ugly? On the contrary, people dare not look it in the eyes, in the same way as they would not dare raise their eyes to look at their king or their deity. Do you want proof? A curse in the context of religion is the counterpart of a dirty joke in the context of love. Reason is held under the spell of a superstition dating back a thousand years to the darkest era of the barbarians. But on this superstition rest the *three barbaric forms of life* that I was talking about: the prostitute hounded like a wild animal out of human society; the old maid condemned to be a physical and spiritual cripple, cheated of her whole love-life; and the untouched young woman jealously guarded with a view to making the most advantageous marriage possible. I hoped by means of this axiom to kindle the pride of women and win them over to fight on my side. For I hoped that women who had realized this and who had dispensed with the prospect of a comfortable life without any worries would show a passionate enthusiasm for my ideal of a beautiful world.

Nothing costs less than moral indignation. A cultivated audience – its composition assured by the taste of theatre directors as well as by the vigilance of the police – scorns cheap means of self-defence. It renounces the opportunity of being able to applaud its own respectability. This feeling of respectability – the feeling of being morally superior to the rogues and sirens assembled on the stage – is so firmly entrenched that only the ostentatious feel the need to display it. But they also want to show the playwright how superior to him they are. This, however, could never prevent us from being proud of the almost super-human trouble we have taken to show our respect for such a strong, courageous playwright. For in him, as in no other writer, the psychological lacerations left by the whip of experience have transformed themselves into furrows ready to receive the seed of poetic creativity.

Die Büchse der Pandora originally published in *Fackel* Nr. 182, June 9 1905, reprinted in *Literatur und Lüge*, Munich 1929
Translated by Celia Skrine

Document 2:   The case of *Pandora's Box* (1905)

**(From the judgment passed by the
Berlin Royal District Court)**

Basing its judgment on the impression it has formed for itself, the
court has come to the conclusion that those readers of this publication whose perception of propriety and impropriety in sexual
matters are in accordance with those prevailing today in educated
and mature circles of German society – indeed, as regards offerings
of this questionable kind, those prevailing amongst the vast majority of German people as a whole (since the book is now on sale and
available to them, too) – will feel their sense of morals and decorum
outraged by the whole content of this publication; in so far as they
have read it, they will have been offended by having been caused to
feel disgust, revulsion, even nausea; and those who have yet to read
it will have the same reactions. The court has been brought to this
conclusion not by the *fact* that the book presents characters whose
manner of thinking, speaking and acting in sexual matters is
shameless and depraved, but by the manner and *contexts* in which
this depravity is presented.

In Act I the sexual element does not come to the fore in an
obtrusive or embarrassing way until the end. But at the (admittedly
short) end, the enactment of the murder by Lulu of Dr Schön, her
husband and former lover and benefactor, is immediately followed
by the intimation of imminent sexual relations between the murderess and the murdered man's son (who knows about the murder), at
the very scene of the crime. This immediate juxtaposition
violates 'normal' and surely healthy reactions in a most painful way.

The second act, taken independently, lacks all tragic stature or
apparent purpose, and submits the reader to a quite inexhaustible
flow of sexual filth.

To be specific, this consists of: the conversations between Piani
and Lulu on the subject of her introduction into the brothel and the
instructions he gives her on the sexual conduct expected of her
there, the report of the brothel-keeper, Lulu's conversation with

Countess Geschwitz on the latter's sexual perversions, the depiction of how Rodrigo is encouraged into sexual relations with the lesbian Geschwitz and she with him, how he rouses himself by animal means before intercourse, the way in which it is planned that Schigolch shall be financially rewarded for Rodrigo's murder, the introduction of the twelve-year-old child into these depraved surroundings and its willingness to participate in illicit relations. The impression these components create is not counterbalanced by the depiction of any alternative or by any element of amusement, pain, pity, or any other emotions; they are therefore fit only to arouse revulsion or indeed, for the most part, abhorrence as regards sexual matters.

Whether or not the drama is technically competent is a question which may be left open.

Even if it is, satisfaction on this point is not enough to remove from its overall effect the sense of repugnance, revulsion and indeed nausea as regards sexual matters.

This effect renders the publication obscene.

Reprinted in Frank Wedekind, *Die Büchse der Pandora*,
Berlin 1906
Translated by Celia Skrine

Document 3: On the *Pandora's Box* case (1906)

FRANK WEDEKIND

The tragic central character of this play is not Lulu, as the judge erroneously assumed, but Countess Geschwitz. Except in a few isolated episodes, Lulu's role is an entirely passive one in all three acts; the Countess Geschwitz, on the other hand, shows evidence in Act I of what I would not hesitate to call an act of superhuman self-sacrifice. In Act II she is forced by the course of the action to attempt to overcome the terrible curse of sexual abnormality weighing on her, by summoning up all her spiritual strength; after which, in Act III, having borne the most appalling mental torments with stoical resignation, she voluntarily goes to her death in order to protect her friend.

The choice of a character weighed down by the terrible curse of abnormality as the subject of a serious work of dramatic literature was not declared unacceptable in any of the three judgments passed on the play. One must remember that in classical Greek tragedy the central characters are almost always beyond the bounds of normal nature. They are of the lineage of Tantalus; the gods have bound a band of bronze around their brow. This means that despite immense spiritual advances, such as would enable anyone watching their struggle to achieve the greatest human happiness, they can never succeed in freeing themselves from the fearful inherited curse which rules their lives; useless to human society, and passing through appalling suffering, they go alone and wretched to their fate. Abnormality as such could not be branded in a manner more horrifying to the spectator's sensibilities. If, nonetheless, the spectator derives aesthetic pleasure and undisputed spiritual enrichment from such a spectacle, then this raises the dramatic experience from the realm of morality to that of art.

However, the curse of abnormality would not have been sufficient in itself to tempt me to choose it as the subject-matter for a dramatic work. My choice was made more because, as far as I could ascertain, this tragic destiny had not yet received any dramatic treatment in the context of our contemporary culture. Seeing this powerful tragic situation of a human being undergoing spiritual agonies which are exceptionally great yet totally fruitless, I was filled with the urge to rescue it from the fate of being thought ridiculous, and to awaken the sympathy and pity of all those not suffering from it. It seemed to me necessary, as one of the most effective means of achieving my aim, to show the crude mockery and braying derision that are the uneducated man's response to this tragic situation, and to clothe them in as expressive a form as possible. To this end I created the figure of the 'strong man' Rodrigo Quast. Rodrigo Quast is the antagonist of Countess Geschwitz. While working on the play I was fully aware that the mental development forced on Countess Geschwitz by her misfortunes was bound to be lifted higher and higher in moral terms in proportion to how brutally I formulated the wisecracks of this 'strong man'. It was perfectly clear to me that these wisecracks must be constantly defused and overshadowed by the seriousness with which I was treating Countess Geschwitz's fate, and that at the end this tragic seriousness must unquestionably win the day if the play is to achieve its aims . . .

[Wedekind then gives a résumé of the judgments of the courts and of the courts' dispute as to whether the 'normal' reader would appreciate the intended tragic effect of the play.]

There is one more reason why I mention this supposedly normal case in discussing the judgment passed on the original version of my play: this is the difference between middle-class morality, which the judge is called upon to defend, and human morality, which defies any attempt to pass temporal judgment on it. In all three of the judgments passed on the play, commercialized love is dismissively labelled as immoral and its practice a sexual offence. From the standpoint of middle-class morality this label is perfectly correct. But venerable poets of all periods, from King Eudraka (in 'Das irdene Wägelchen', 'The little earthen carriage') to Goethe (in 'Der Gott und die Bajadere', 'The God and the Bayadere') have felt impelled to defend prostitution against being judged in this way. And Jesus said to the chief priests and judges of his day: 'I tell you truly, the tax-collectors and the prostitutes are entering the kingdom of God ahead of you' (Matthew 21: 31). From his point of view Jesus could not speak more logically or more consistently, for the kingdom of God he promises is for those that labour and are heavily laden, not for the rich; for the sick, not the healthy; for sinners, not for the righteous.

But, I hear the judge ask, if those who labour, the sick and the sinners, are justified by this moral system, does this not lead deplorably to the destruction of culture? I can give answers to this question enough to allay any anxiety; for if human morality desires to be placed higher than bourgeois morality, then it must also be based on a deeper and more universal knowledge of the world and of human nature. But, unless expressly ordered to do so, I shall not take upon myself the task of defending before the judge the pronouncements of the founder of our religion.

Frank Wedekind, *Die Büchse der Pandora*, Berlin 1906
Translated by Celia Skrine

Document 4:   A note on Act III of *Lulu*

GEORGE PERLE

In 1936, Acts I and II of *Lulu* were published in a piano-vocal score prepared by Erwin Stein,[1] with a prefatory note by the publisher stating that Berg had completed the composition of the three-act opera shortly before his death, that he had completed the orchestration of the first two acts and of portions of the third, and that publication of Act III would follow. It was generally assumed at the time that the orchestration of Act III would be completed by a colleague of Berg's. The engraving of Stein's reduction of Act III was actually begun, but never completed, presumably because political conditions in 1937 made this impossible. In 1953 the original (piano-vocal) edition was reprinted without the prefatory note mentioned above. In performance, the third act has always been presented in an adaptation consisting of fragments from a symphonic suite derived by Berg from the opera, and of several lines from the libretto, converted into ordinary speech.

Beginning in 1959, when I was working on my analysis of *Lulu*,[2] I had naturally been deeply interested in examining the unpublished portions of Act III, but was for a long time unsuccessful in my efforts to be granted permission to do so. In the summer of 1963, however, I was finally able to obtain permission through the kindness of Dr Alfred Kalmus. In approaching this material, I was concerned with the considerable speculation that has arisen, as a result of the continuing non-completion of the orchestration and of the non-publication of the piano-vocal score of Act III as originally announced, that the material left by Berg at his death is so fragmentary as to present formidable obstacles to the realization of these projects. I am herewith publishing my report to Dr Kalmus in the hope that it will dispel such speculation by establishing once for all the feasibility of preparing the score so that an authentic performance of the complete work will at last be possible.

August 21, 1963

Dr Alfred A. Kalmus
Universal Edition
2/3, Fareham Street
London, W.1

Dear Dr Kalmus:

Here is the summary which you suggested that I submit to you, reporting my conclusions regarding the Berg material that you kindly arranged for me to study in Vienna earlier this month.

With the exception of not more than twenty bars in Act III, Scene 2, which are almost but not entirely completed, the third act of *Lulu* is complete, both musically and dramatically, including the full orchestration of three-fifths of Scene 2 and almost the same proportion of Scene 1.

First of all, let us consider the few 'incomplete' bars. These are found within mm. 952–980 (my measure numbers follow Stein's correction of Berg's erroneous measure numbers), the concluding section of a vocal quartet beginning at m. 938. This section is a recapitulation of the 'Hymne' with which Act II concludes, omitting the original introduction (mm. 1097–1150), conclusion (mm. 1142–1150), and intermediate sections in new tempi (mm. 1112–1130 and 1136–1138). In the recapitulation the orchestral music and Alwa's solo are complete. But as a background to Alwa's solo here, Berg intended to continue a conversation, already begun, between Lulu, Geschwitz, and Schigolch. This background is indicated by Berg in a fragment of text, several notes without text, and brackets indicating exactly where one, two, or all three of the accompanying singers are to appear. In a marginal note Berg indicates the source (page and line) in Wedekind for the missing lines of text. In the completed portion of the vocal quartet, mm. 938–951, the vocal lines are derived by doubling linear details already present in the orchestral part; and of course, this would be the technique required to fill in the few missing notes in mm. 952–980. With the assistance of the suggestions provided by Berg himself, I cannot see why a satisfactory solution should require more than a few hours of work. As a matter of fact, I should guess that Berg himself, finding that he had not left sufficient space for filling in the missing details when he returned to this passage at some later date, probably completed them on a separate sheet. My supposition is based on the fact that Berg had apparently completed every other musical, textual, and dramatic detail of the *Particell* by the time he undertook the task of laying out the full score.

Berg's *Particell* is not in any sense a 'sketch'. It is, on the contrary, a final statement of the music and text, indicating (with the negligible exceptions mentioned above) every note of music, every metronome mark, every word of text, and every stage direction, preparatory to the final realization of the work in full score. The question that remains, then, is what must still be done in order to complete the full score?

Of the 590 measures comprised in Scene 2 (mm. 715–1304), more than 330 can be laid out in full score *exactly* according to Berg's intentions. Measures 715–730 and 805–820 present a tremolo string passage against which the 'Procurer's Song' (Wedekind's own tune) appears. The stage directions say, 'Eine Drehorgel spielt hinter der Szene.' The exact manner in which the *Drehorgel* music is to be realized for these 32 bars is shown in the Variation movement of the *Lulu-Suite*, from the upbeat to m. 45 through m. 48. Other portions of the Variation movement (which appears in the opera as the intermezzo between III/1 and III/2) are literally restated in III/2 at mm. 1002–1025 (Var., mm. 17–27) and at mm. 1088–1097 (Var., mm. 33–37 and 29–32). Practically all of the final movement of the Suite appears in III/2, as follows:

III/2   Adagio, from the Suite

1124–1164 = 0–40
1213–1235 = 44–63
1272–1304 = 78–110

There are thus 173 bars of Scene 2 which Berg himself orchestrated in the Variations and Finale of the Suite. The exact scoring which Berg intended for an approximately equal additional number of bars becomes evident once the dramatic plan of III/2 is understood.[3]

In a final draft, such as Berg's manuscript represents, one expects to see copious explicit instrumental indications. It is, at first sight, surprising to find that there are extensive portions of the *Particell* which lack these indications. But a closer study in relation to the work as a whole reveals Berg's explicit intentions regarding the exact orchestration of these passages beyond any reasonable doubt. In fact, Berg omits instrumental indications because the exact scoring of these passages has already been determined and can be reconstructed easily without the aid of such indications.

In a letter which Berg wrote to Schoenberg while he was still occupied with the preparation of the libretto (see Redlich's *Alban Berg*, p. 218)[4] he mentions his plan of having Lulu's clients in the last scene played by the same performers who had played the parts of Lulu's victims in the first half of the opera. The final realization of this plan, whose details differ from those that Berg had described in his letter to Schoenberg four years earlier, requires that the succession of victims in Acts I and II and the succession of clients in the final scene be exactly parallel, the *Medizinalrat* returning as the Professor, the Painter as the Negro, and Dr Schoen as Jack (cf. Reich, *Alban Berg*, p. 111). Not only are the vocal requirements for each pair of characters identical (the *Medizinalrat* and the Professor do not sing, the Painter and the Negro call for a lyrical tenor, and Dr Schoen and Jack require a *Heldenbariton*), but each of the two corresponding roles is also compositionally characterized by identical musical material. But beyond this, each of the supposedly new characters brings with him a literal return of complete musical episodes associated with his counterpart in the first half of the opera.

Thus the entrance of Lulu and the Professor brings with it the music of that section of I/1 in which Lulu is present with the corpse of the *Medizinalrat*, the male role being an entirely silent one in both instances – a recapitulation of the *Recitativ* (Act I, mm. 284–292) and two recapitulations of the *Canzonetta* (Act I, mm. 262–283); with the entrance of Lulu and the Negro, there are recapitulations of musical episodes associated with the Painter – sections of the *Monoritmica* of Act I, the beginning of the *Duettino* with which Act I, Scene 2 opens, and the first strophe of the *Duett* (Act I, mm. 305–312); with the entrance of Lulu and Jack there are two recapitulations of the *Kavatine*, Act II, mm. 61–72, and a recapitulation of the Intermezzo between I/2 and I/3, which is based on the melody of Dr Schoen's words at the very end of Act I, 'Jetzt kommt die Hinrichtung.'

The inclusion of this Intermezzo from Act I in the final movement of the *Lulu-Suite*, which is otherwise limited to extracts from Act III, Scene 2, is one among several proofs that the recapitulations of earlier numbers as just described above are intended to repeat the original orchestration of these earlier numbers. Other evidence is the almost total absence of instrumental indications in these recapitulatory sections of the *Particell* (such indications would certainly have been present, to some extent, had Berg intended to revise the original orchestration of these sections). A third proof is found in the fact that these returns are very largely literal in all other respects, except for the vocal parts and text, of course. Such changes as occur are mainly notational ones. For example, in order to accommodate a given quotation from an earlier scene within a tempo that is approximately twice as fast as that of the original, it will appear in the recapitulation in note values that are twice those of the original. Finally, and apart from the above extrinsic evidence, the logic of both the musical and the dramatic structure of the work as a whole requires a return to the orchestration of the expository statement of each of the passages in question.

There are, then, about 350 bars in III/2 which have already been fully[5] orchestrated by Berg himself. While we cannot know *exactly* how Berg might have orchestrated the remaining two-fifths of Scene 2, the orchestration of these remaining passages in a manner consistent with what he himself would have done presents no problems whatever, for the following reasons:

1 Each of the remaining sections is surrounded by material the scoring of which was completed by Berg himself.
2 Instrumental indications are found in the *Particell*.
3 No new material whatever is found in these sections. On the contrary, they are entirely based on characteristic harmonic, rhythmic, and melodic ideas associated with Alwa, Geschwitz, Schigolch, and Lulu. Extensive sections based on the same material will be found throughout the opera, particularly in Act II, from which their equally characteristic timbres can be deduced.
4 Additional recapitulations of early numbers will be found among these unscored sections of III/2, which I have not included in the above list of recapitulated numbers because they are less literal. Nevertheless, the original numbers are full of valuable suggestions for the scoring of these modified recapitulations. An example is the 'Hymne', discussed at the beginning of this letter.

Of the 670 bars in Act III, Scene 1, the first 268 were completed in full score by Berg. This includes the Introduction and first Ensemble, the long duet between Lulu and the Marquis, and the second

Ensemble. The third (final) Ensemble incorporates in their entirety the orchestral parts of the first and second Ensembles, thus providing the full orchestration of more than 50 additional bars.[6] Mm. 448–476, entitled *Cadenz*, is limited to a duet for solo violin and solo piano. The instrumentation of the 12 bars following this duet is also precisely given. There are, therefore, not less than 360 bars of III/1 which may be said to have been fully scored, in every detail, by Berg himself.[7] As in the case of III/2, the orchestration of the remaining two-fifths of Scene 1 in a manner consistent with the sections orchestrated by Berg presents no difficulties whatever.

May I call to your attention the fact that many of the points that I have made above were already made some years ago by Dr Redlich in his book (pp. 265ff.), where he emphasizes the necessity and feasibility of completing Berg's masterpiece. I would go so far as to say that it is an error to speak of another person 'completing' *Lulu*, for in every essential respect this has already been done by Alban Berg. I cannot see how anyone who has studied Berg's own version of Act III can regard the present makeshift substitute that is employed in performances of the opera as anything less than an egregious and unnecessary distortion of his work, one which even falsifies retroactively the music and drama of the first and second acts. Act III, Scene 1, I regard as not only the high point of the opera as a whole and the climax of Berg's entire creative career, but as an artistic achievement that is unmatched in all of operatic literature.

Sincerely yours,
George Perle

Originally published in *Perspectives of New Music*, vol. 2, no. 2 (Spring/Summer, 1964): 8–13.

Editorial note

The truth of many of the ideas and suggestions put forward in this, the second of George Perle's published writings on *Lulu*, have been corroborated by subsequent research.

In preparing the original version of his completion of Act III Friedrich Cerha was prevented by the restrictions imposed by the composer's widow from studying all the Berg material in the Austrian National Library. Since Berg's marginal notes did not provide sufficient text for the Quartet of Act III, scene 2, Cerha was obliged to draw on a passage earlier in the Wedekind play to arrive at additional text of his own invention (a decision which Perle later criticised in his otherwise enthusiastic review of the Cerha score[8]). It is this version of the text of the Quartet that appears in the published vocal score of Act III.

The speculation in the above article that Berg himself probably completed the text of the Quartet on a sheet of paper that had become separated from the Particell was, however, confirmed in 1981 when Perle discovered the missing text amongst the material in the Austrian National Library.[9] By this time Cerha had also had access to this material[10] and it is his revised version of the Quartet, with Berg's own text, that appears in the more recently published orchestral score of Act III.

Berg's use of double and treble roles in *Lulu*, outlined above and originally put forward in Perle's first *Lulu* article[11] was subsequently verified by my own study of Berg's sketches;[12] these double and treble roles, largely ignored in the first published score of the opera, are now incorporated in the new vocal and orchestral scores of Act III.

The implication in the above article that the orchestration of Act III presents no special problems and the suggestion that the unorchestrated passages that recapitulate earlier material should, wherever possible, simply repeat Berg's own earlier scoring has not been adopted by Cerha and represents something of an oversimplification of the situation – a case of special pleading motivated by the fact that at the time the article was written 'it seemed better to emphasize solutions, even questionable ones, rather than problems'.

Document 5: The 'lost' score of the *Symphonic Pieces* from *Lulu*

DOUGLAS JARMAN

The chronological catalogue of Berg's compositions which Redlich published in his 1957 book on Berg[1] includes a horrifyingly large number of works the manuscripts of which are described as 'lost'. Although subsequent research and, in particular, the recent publication of a catalogue of the Berg manuscripts in the Musiksammlung of the Österreichische Nationalbibliothek have shown that most of the manuscripts which Redlich feared lost do, in fact, exist and are now in safe hands, there appears to be at least one manuscript that has disappeared since Redlich compiled his catalogue.

According to Redlich, all the *Lulu* manuscripts were, in 1957, in the possession of Helene Berg. Under the heading '*Symphonic Pieces from "Lulu"*' in Rosemary Hilmar's recent catalogue[2] – a catalogue compiled since the death of Helene Berg and including all the manuscripts which, originally in her possession, are now in the Österreichische Nationalbibliothek – there appear only the following five entries:

(1) a sketch of the selection of movements in the *Symphonic Pieces*
(2) a sketch of the arrangements of the pieces
(3) a sketch of the title page and a list of corrections to the score
(4) a list of queries from Apostel to Berg and Berg's replies
(5) a copy of the published score of the *Symphonic Pieces*

If, as Redlich believed, the *Lulu* manuscripts were in Helene Berg's possession, why is the autograph manuscript of the *Symphonic Pieces* not amongst those that are now deposited in the Nationalbibliothek? Can the manuscript of so important a work have disappeared? Friedrich Cerha, in his monograph on Act III of *Lulu*, confirms one's fears that this might, indeed, be the case. Cerha, quite unequivocally, states that the manuscript is lost and has been so for some considerable time:

125

The score of the last two movements of the *Symphonic Pieces*, which with the exception of a few bars ... are contained literally in Act III, is published. It is not possible to check the texts for their authenticity because the autograph score is now lost. The last information about the score is a note with Universal Edition, according to which it had been returned – presumably after the preparation of the orchestral material – to Herr Berg. There is no evidence that Hans Erich Apostel had the original score of the *Symphonic Pieces* at his disposal when revising the opera.[3]

Happily, Cerha is mistaken. The autograph score of the *Symphonic Pieces* exists and is available to anyone interested in checking the authenticity of the published score – indeed, was available for study even before the manuscripts in Helene Berg's possession were transferred to the Nationalbibliothek in 1976. The manuscript lies in the Musiksammlung of the ÖNB but in a place where no one has thought to look.

Berg began work on the final scene of *Lulu* in January or February of 1935. By 4 March he had reached somewhere around m. 1090 of the published vocal score[4] and finished the composition of the whole opera in April. The following month Berg wrote to U.E., outlining his plan for putting together a 'propaganda suite' from the music of *Lulu* and began work on the orchestration by first scoring those sections of the opera that were to be included in this suite, the *Symphonic Pieces from 'Lulu'*. Having completed and sent off the autograph score of the *Symphonic Pieces* early in the summer of 1934, Berg then went back to the beginning of the opera and scored the rest of the work consecutively. When, in due course, U.E. returned the autograph manuscript of the *Pieces* to him, Berg saved himself both time and trouble by simply absorbing the manuscript of the already scored sections into the body of the full score. The autograph manuscript of the *Symphonic Pieces from 'Lulu'* thus exists not as a separate entity but as a part of the full score of the opera itself.

Some movements from the *Symphonic Pieces* could be integrated into the full score of the opera without much difficulty. All that was necessary to convert the manuscript of the *Ostinato* movement of the *Pieces* into the manuscript of the *Ostinato* Film Music interlude at the centre of Act II, for example, was to cover the opening page of the original manuscript (that is to say bars 1–6 of the *Ostinato* of the *Symphonic Pieces*, which do not appear in the opera) with a new sheet of manuscript on which were written mm. 652–55 of Act II. Once this new lead into the Film Music from Act II, sc. I, and a similar lead out of the interlude into Act II, sc. 2, had been arranged, the manuscript of the *Ostinato* of the *Symphonic Pieces* could be inserted in its entirety into the full score of the opera. The manuscript of the *Lied der Lulu* (although written on smaller sized manuscript than the rest of the opera score – on 18 as opposed to 26 staves) could be, and was, similarly inserted bodily into the full score.

Rather than reserve the manuscript of the *Adagio* movement of the *Symphonic Pieces* until he was orchestrating the final scene of the opera, Berg absorbed the larger part of it into the full score of Act I. A comparison of the *Adagio* of the *Symphonic Pieces* with the relevant passages in Act III of *Lulu* shows that, although they share the same music, the two are frequently quite distinct in both notation and tempo. At mm. 45ff. of the *Adagio* of the *Pieces*, for example, Dr Schön's Coda theme appears notated in 4/4 and with a metronome marking of ♩ = 38; in the last scene of the opera itself, on the other hand, this same music appears (mm. 1244ff.) with a metronome marking of ♩ = 58 and notated in 3/4. In fact, the passage from m. 45ff. of the *Adagio* corresponds notationally and in its metronome marking with the appearance of this same music as the orchestral interlude between scenes 2 and 3 of Act I; it was here, in the full score of the First Act, that Berg inserted mm. 44–73 of the manuscript of the *Adagio*. Consequently, despite the fact that Berg never wrote the full score of the final scene of Act III, there is no separate existing score of the *Adagio* of the *Symphonic Pieces*.

If the manuscripts of the *Ostinato* and the *Lied der Lulu* from the *Pieces* could be easily inserted into the full score of the opera, the absorption of the manuscript of the *Rondo* presented greater difficulties. In the opera, the exposition of Alwa's rondo in Act II, sc. 1 is continually interrupted by the appearance and disappearance of various other characters. In putting together the *Rondo* of the *Symphonic Pieces*, Berg had simply excised the music which accompanies these interruptions and had brought together the different sections of Alwa's music to form a continuous, unbroken movement. In attempting to absorb the manuscript of the *Rondo* movement into the full score of the opera, Berg was faced with the task of dismantling the score of the *Symphonic Pieces* in order to re-insert the omitted passages. He solved the problem with considerable ingenuity.

Putting aside the first sheet of the manuscript of the *Rondo* from the *Pieces*, Berg took the second sheet (which had mm. 9–15 on one side and mm. 16–18 on the reverse), turned it round, and taped it into the full score. He then glued a new sheet of manuscript paper over the reverse side of the original sheet (that is, over mm. 16–18). The new sheet, which formed p. 41 of the full score of Act II, had written on it mm. 239–42 of the opera; its reverse (p. 42) had on it mm. 9–15 of the original *Rondo* manuscript which thus became mm. 243–49 of the full score. A double sheet of manuscript (pp. 43/44 and 45/46), on which were written the bars of the interpolated interruption (mm. 250–61) and the three following bars of the *Rondo* (the now hidden mm. 16–18 of the *Rondo* from the *Pieces*, which became mm. 262–64 of Act II), was then inserted before the next sheet of the manuscript of the *Symphonic Pieces* was added. The following diagram shows the pagination of this section of the full score. The encircled numbers are those of the pages in the full score. The bar numbers in square brackets refer to bar numbers in the *Rondo* movement of the *Symphonic Pieces*; pages which have these bar numbers are those of the original manuscript of the *Symphonic Pieces*. The unbracketed bar numbers are those of Act II of the complete opera.

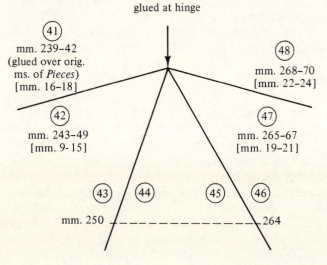

Fig. 2

The next four double-sided pages of the full score are a similar compilation of pages from the original manuscript of the *Symphonic*

Pieces and inserted sheets. The layout of these pages is shown in the following diagram. Pages 53 and 54 of the full score, which have on them the music that accompanies the entrance of the Manservant at mm. 287ff. of Act II, are a single sheet taped into the manuscript of the movement from the *Symphonic Pieces*. The new page 53 has on it mm. 284–86 which correspond to mm. 37–39 of the *Rondo* of the *Pieces*, and these bars of the original manuscript are covered by a pasted-on sheet (p. 55), allowing for Dr Schön's exclamation at mm. 293–97, before the original manuscript reappears as p. 56. A similar new sheet is pasted over the original manuscript of mm. 26–27 to allow for the inclusion of the additional 'tumultuoso' bar (m. 274) on p. 49.

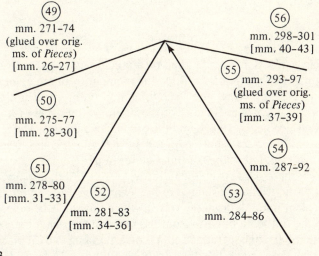

Fig. 3

The remaining four pages of the full score of Act II, sc. 1, which include the music of Alwa's Rondo, are organized in a similar way:

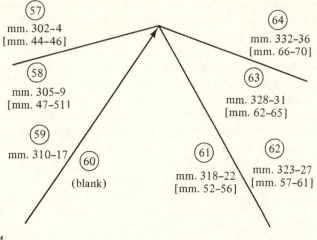

Fig. 4

Pages 57, 58, 61, 62, 63, and 64 are made up of pages from the original manuscript of the *Rondo* movement from the *Symphonic Pieces*. Berg wrote the 'subito tumultuoso' interruption at mm. 310–17 of Act II, sc. 1 of the opera on one side of a single sheet which he then taped into the original manuscript. The reverse side of this sheet (that is, p. 60) he left blank apart from the handwritten note: 'Leer (erfüllet dieser in der Kopie).'

That these pages from the full score of Act II did, initially, form part of the *Rondo* movement of the *Symphonic Pieces from 'Lulu'* is evident not only from the way in which they have been inserted into the full score but also from the fact that they bear two sets of bar numbers: one set (added later) corresponding to their placing in the complete opera, the other (rubbed out but still clearly legible) corresponding to their placing in the *Symphonic Pieces*. The numbering of the bars of the Rondo in accordance with their position in the *Symphonic Pieces* ends at m. 336 of the full score of Act II, sc. 1 (that is, at m. 70 of the *Rondo* of the *Pieces*) and restarts at m. 1001 of Act II, sc. 2 (which is numbered m. 71), the point at which Alwa's *Rondo* reappears and the *Rondo* of the *Symphonic Pieces* takes up the music once more. Similarly, the manuscript of the orchestral interlude between scenes 2 and 3 of Act I in the full score bears bar numbers which indicate the point at which this music appears in the *Adagio* of the *Symphonic Pieces* and bar numbers that are supposed to correspond to those of the complete opera – 'supposed to' because, in this case, Berg made a mistake when counting the number of bars and the passage is incorrectly numbered mm. 874–906.[5] The Film Music *Ostinato* interlude also has two sets of bar numbers.

As final proof that these pages of the autograph full score constitute the original autograph score of the *Symphonic Pieces* also, there are, in both the manuscripts of the *Ostinato* and the *Lied der Lulu*, instructions to Wolf, the copyist who prepared the score of the *Symphonic Pieces*, as to how the score was to be laid out. Thus at mm. 685–89 of Act II, for example (that is at mm. 35–39 of the *Ostinato* of the *Symphonic Pieces*, the turning point of the palindromic Film Music) Berg has written:

Wolf: Bitte die Takte (35) 36, 37, 38 (39) ebenso symmetrisch auslegen.

Wolf followed this instruction and the page is, as Berg requested, laid out symmetrically around the central bar of the palindrome in the published score of the *Symphonic Pieces from 'Lulu'*. Berg's instructions are only partially observed in the layout of the same passage in the published full score of the opera.

In the complete *Lulu* the remaining, and as yet unmentioned, movement of the *Symphonic Pieces* – the *Variationen* – forms the orchestral interlude between the two scenes of Act III. Although Berg never finished orchestrating the first scene of the Act, the autograph score of the *Variations* is in its place at the centre of the unfinished full score of Act III.[6]

Once it is realized that these parts of the full score of *Lulu* began life as the autograph score of the *Symphonic Pieces*, it becomes possible to explain some of the more puzzling aspects of both the manuscript and the published miniature score of the opera. At m. 964 of Act I and m. 1144 of Act II of the published score, for example, the vibraphone part is doubled by the piano 'falls kein Vibraphon vorhanden ist'. This doubling is meaningless in the context of the whole opera since the vibraphone is required throughout the piece. Like other such doublings in the score, this has been taken over literally from the score of the *Symphonic Pieces* or from what was to have been the score of the longer *Lulu Symphony*, which Berg planned and upon which he presumably began work before abandoning the idea.[7] Clearly, a vibraphone, which is a necessity when the whole of *Lulu* is to be performed, might well be regarded as a luxury when the *Symphonic Pieces* are to be performed separately as a single item in a whole concert.

Whether knowingly or not, Apostel did have the score of the *Symphonic Pieces* at his disposal when he prepared the full score of the opera and, since Berg had not found time to get rid of the now unnecessary doublings of the *Pieces*, they were transferred without revision into the score of the opera.

Originally published in the *International Alban Berg Society Newsletter*, vol. 12 (Fall/Winter, 1982): 14–16.

Notes

1. Introduction: chronology and background

1 Donald Harris, 'Berg and Miss Frida', *Alban Berg Symposion*, ed. Rudolf Klein, Alban Berg Studien II, Vienna, Universal Edition, 1981, p. 200.
2 Stefan Zweig, *The World of Yesterday*, London, Cassell, 1943, p. 45.
3 Willi Reich, *Alban Berg*, trans. Cornelius Cardew, London, Thames and Hudson, 1965, p. 22.
4 Alban Berg, *Letters to his Wife*, London, Faber and Faber, 1971, p. 24.
5 J. Brand, C. Hailey and D. Harris, *The Berg–Schoenberg Correspondence*, New York, Norton, 1987 p. 366.
6 *Ibid.*, p. 368.
7 *Ibid.*, p. 369.
8 Rosemary Hilmar, *Katalog der Musikhandschriften, Schriften und Studien Alban Bergs*, Alban Berg Studien I, Vienna, Universal Edition, 1980, p. 27, Cat. No. 45.
9 The same sketch is discussed by Volker Scherliess ('Alban Bergs analytische Tafeln zur Lulu-Reihe', *Die Musik Forschung* 4, October–December 1977, pp. 452–64) and by Patricia Hall ('The Progress of a Method; Berg's Tone-Rows for *Lulu*', *Musical Quarterly* 71, 1985, No. 4, p. 500).
10 Berg to Webern in the files of Universal Edition. For a discussion of the chronology of Berg's developing of the different row forms see Patricia Hall, 'The Progress of a Method'.
11 J. Brand, C. Hailey and D. Harris, *The Berg–Schoenberg Correspondence*, p. 433.
12 Alban Berg to Webern, 15 September 1933 (the files of Universal Edition).
13 Berg, *Letters to His Wife*, p. 421.
14 This poster is reproduced on the cover of the *Österreichische Musikzeitschrift*, No. 4, 1988.
15 See Douglas Jarman, *Alban Berg 'Wozzeck'*, Cambridge, Cambridge University Press, 1989, pp. 76–7.
16 John Russell, *Erich Kleiber*, London, André Deutsch, 1957, p. 140.
17 Eva Adensamer, 'Bergs geistige Umgebung – Briefe aus seinem Nachlass', *Alban Berg Symposion*, ed. Rudolf Klein, Alban Berg Studien II, Vienna, Universal Edition, 1981, p. 187.

18 Russell, *Erich Kleiber*, p. 143.
19 *Ibid.*, p. 143.
20 *Ibid.*, pp. 143–4.
21 See Nicholas Slonimsky, *Music since 1900* (4th edition), Cassell, London, 1971, p. 595.
22 *Ibid.*, p. 596.
23 Vera Lampert, 'Schoenbergs, Bergs und Adornos Briefe an Sándor Jemnitz', *Studia Musicologica Academiae Scientiarum Hungaricae*, 13, 1973, pp. 363–4.
24 Willi Reich, 'Erich Kleiber und Alban Berg', *Schweizerische Musikzeitschrift* 98, 1952, pp. 376–7.
25 Hans Redlich, *Versuch einer Würdigung*, Vienna, Universal Edition, 1957, p. 401.
26 Louis Krasner, 'The Origins of the Berg Violin Concerto', *Alban Berg Symposion*, ed. Rudolf Klein, Vienna, Universal Edition, 1981, p. 108.
27 Reich, *Alban Berg*, 1965, p. 103.
28 Private letter to the author.
29 Unpublished letter from Webern to Schoenberg, 23 January 1936.
30 Volker Scherliess, *Alban Berg*, Hamburg, Rowohlt Taschenbuch, 1976, p. 133.
31 Paul A. Pisk, 'Personal Recollections of Alban Berg', *Newsletter of the International Alban Berg Society*, No. 10, Summer 1981, p. 12.
32 Unpublished letter from Webern to Schoenberg, 23 January 1936.
33 *Ibid*.

2. From play to libretto

1 Heinrich Mann quoted in *Frank Wedekind: Gedichte und Chansons*, Frankfurt, Fischer Bücherei, 1968, p. 154.
2 Bertolt Brecht quote in Frederic Ewen, *Bertolt Brecht: His Life, his Art and his Times*, London, Calder and Boyards, 1970, p. 66.
3 Robert Gittleman, *Frank Wedekind*, New York, Twayne, 1968, p. 22.
4 Franz Schoenberner, *Confessions of a European Intellectual*, New York, Collier Books, 1965, pp. 313–14.
5 Robert Gittleman, *Wedekind*, p. 23.
6 Quoted in Gittleman, *Wedekind*, p. 23.
7 *Ibid.*, p. 27.
8 T. W. Adorno, *Alban Berg*, Vienna, Elisabeth Lafite Verlag, 1968, p. 147.
9 Karl Neumann, 'Wedekind and Berg's *Lulu*', *Music Review* 35, February 1975, p. 52.
10 *Ibid.*, p. 52.
11 Robert Gittleman, *Wedekind*, p. 134.
12 J. Brand, C. Hailey and D. Harris, *The Berg–Schoenberg Correspondence*, p. 134.
13 Karl Neumann, 'Wedekind and Berg's *Lulu*', p. 47. David Drew has also pointed out the similarity between Berg's use of a silent film to chart the progress of his heroine and Weill's similar prior use in his opera *Royal*

Palace. See David Drew, 'Musical Theatre in the Weimar Republic', *Proceedings of the Royal Musical Association* 88, 1962, p. 193.
14 J. Brand, C. Hailey and D. Harris, *The Berg–Schoenberg Correspondence*, p. 405.
15 The handwritten copy in the British Library (reproduced in Plate 2) heads the fair copy of the Prologue which Berg sent to Schoenberg in September 1934 as a sixtieth birthday present. The second (typewritten) copy is amongst the sketches for *Lulu* in the possession of the Music Department of the Austrian National Library.
16 George Perle, *The Operas of Alban Berg*, Vol. II: *Lulu*, Berkeley, University of California Press, 1985, p. 62.
17 Karl Neumann, 'Wedekind and Berg's *Lulu*', p. 49.

3. Synopsis

1 George Perle has pointed out that Berg's shooting-script and musical plan for the Film Music Interlude are not consistent with what happens in the following scene since, although Berg indicates that the film shows Lulu and Geschwitz changing places in the isolation hospital it is only in the following scene that we see Geschwitz leaving for the hospital in order to effect this change. (See George Perle, *The Operas of Alban Berg*, Vol. II: *Lulu*, Berkeley, University of California Press, 1985, p. 156.)

4. Posthumous history

1 See Friedrich Cerha, *Arbeitsbericht zur Herstellung des 3. Akts der Oper 'Lulu' von Alban Berg*, Vienna, Universal Edition, 1979.
2 Willi Reich, *Alban Berg*, Vienna, Herbert Reichner Verlag, 1937, p. 124.
3 See Walter Szmolyan, 'Zum III, Akt von Alban Bergs "Lulu"', *Österreichische Musikzeitschrift* 30.11/9, September 1977, p. 398.
4 Friedrich Cerha, *Arbeitsbericht*, p. 36.
5 *Ibid.*, p. 37.
6 *Ibid.*, p. 36.
7 In a letter to George Perle dated 4.1.1977.
8 Thomas Mann, *Diaries 1918–1939*, trans. Richard and Clara Winston, Robin Clark, London, 1984, p. 278.
9 *Schweizerische Musikzeitung* 77, 1937, pp. 385–6.
10 *Die Musik* 29, 1937, p. 271.
11 Friedrich Cerha, *Arbeitsbericht*, p. 38.
12 *Ibid.*, p. 39.
13 *Melos* 16, 1949, p. 121.
14 *New Statesman and Nation*, 27 August 1949, p. 127.
15 *Time and Tide* 34, 1953, p. 1098.
16 Walter Szmolyan, 'Helene Bergs Vermächtnis', *Österreichische Musikzeitschrift* 32.4, April 1977, pp. 169ff.
17 *Melos* 29, 1962, p. 292.
18 Friedrich Cerha, *Arbeitsbericht*, p. 2.

19 The following pages are adapted from my article 'Friedrich's *Lulu*', *Newsletter of the International Alban Berg Society*, Summer 1981.
20 *The Guardian*, 28 February 1979.
21 *The Observer*, 4 March 1979.
22 *The Financial Times*, 28 February 1979.
23 *The Sunday Telegraph*, 4 March 1979.
24 *Opera*, April 1979, pp. 329–30.
25 *The New Yorker*, 5 January 1981 reprinted in *Musical Events*, London, Grafton Books, 1985, p. 92.
26 George Perle, *The Operas of Alban Berg*, Vol. II: *Lulu*, Berkeley, University of California Press, 1985, p. 182.
27 Douglas Jarman, 'Friedrich's *Lulu*'.
28 Pierre Boulez, '*Lulu*: A Short Postscript on Fidelity' in *Orientations*, ed. J. J. Nattiez, trans. Martin Cooper, London, Faber and Faber, 1986, pp. 400–1.
29 *The Guardian*, 17 February 1988.
30 *Die Frankfurter Allgemeine Zeitung*, 2 February 1988.
31 *The Financial Times*, 9 February 1988.
32 Douglas Jarman, *Wozzeck*, Cambridge University Press, 1989, p. 2.
33 *The Guardian*, 23 October 1987.
34 *Music and Musicians*, February 1988.
35 *The Northern Echo*, 13 November 1987.
36 *The Independent*, 24 October 1987.
37 *The Financial Times*, 23 October 1987.

5. The formal design

1 See J. Brand, C. Hailey and D. Harris, *The Berg–Schoenberg Correspondence*, p. 405.
2 See Patricia Hall, 'The Progress of a Method: Berg's Tone Rows for *Lulu*', *Musical Quarterly* 71, 1985, No. 4, pp. 500–19.
3 The dramatic significance of the doubling of the roles of the Animal Trainer and the Athlete (two other characters who again do not share musical material) has been discussed in chapter 2.

6. Melodic, harmonic and rhythmic language

1 Gerald Abraham, *A Hundred Years of Music* (3rd edition), London, Duckworth, 1964, p. 289.
2 The different forms of a twelve-note set are here indicated by the letters 'P', for the prime or original form, and 'I' for the inversion (in Berg's music retrograde forms are rarely employed, and then only for special metaphoric purposes). The most important pitch-level associated with a set is indicated by the figure '0'. Other figures denote transpositions, the number itself indicating the number of semitone steps above this '0' level at which the relevant transposition is to be found.
3 George Perle, *The Operas of Alban Berg*, Vol. II: *Lulu*, Berkeley, University of California Press, 1985, pp. 102–3.
4 The following section is adapted from my article 'Some Observations on

Rhythm, Metre and Tempo in *Lulu'*, *Alban Berg Symposion*, ed. Rudolf Klein, Alban Berg Studien II, Vienna, Universal Edition, 1981, pp. 20ff.
5 Such a book exists in George Perle's comprehensive and authoritative *The Operas of Alban Berg*, Vol. II: *Lulu* to which any reader wishing to pursue the topic is referred.

7. Act III, scene 2, b.1146–1326: an analysis

1 George Perle (*The Operas of Alban Berg*, Vol. II: *Lulu*, Berkeley, University of California Press, 1985, p. 110) has pointed out that the upper line of the Picture chords forms a fragment of the octatonic scale and the progression in these bars thus presents in the upper part statements of the three distinct octatonic scales.
2 *Ibid.*, pp. 128–9.
3 George Perle, 'Some Thoughts on an Ideal Production of *Lulu'*, *The Journal of Musicology*, 7.2, Spring 1989.
4 *Ibid.*, p. 251.
5 George Perle, *The Operas of Alban Berg*, Vol. II: *Lulu*, p. 190.

8. A suggested interpretation

1 Hans Redlich, *Alban Berg*, London, John Calder 1957, p. 113.
2 Bryan Appleyard, *The Culture Club: Crisis in the Arts*, London, Faber and Faber, p. 117.
3 Stefan Zweig, *The World of Yesterday*, London, Cassell, 1943, p. 63.
4 *Ibid.*, p. 70.
5 *Ibid.*, p. 75.
6 *Ibid.*, p. 75.
7 Alban Berg, 'The Problem of Opera' in Willi Reich, *Alban Berg*, London, Thames and Hudson, 1965, p. 64.
8 Max Marschalk, *Vossische Zeitung*, 23 December 1932. For a more extended discussion of the influence of Brecht on Berg see my article 'Weill and Berg: *Lulu* as Epic Opera' in *A New Orpheus*, ed. Kim Kowalke, New Haven, Yale University Press, 1986, pp. 147ff.
9 Kurt Weill, 'Alban Berg: *Wozzeck'* reprinted in *Ausgewählte Schriften*, ed. David Drew, Frankfurt, Suhrkamp Verlag, 1975, p. 152.
10 Kurt Weill, 'Die neue Oper' reprinted in Kim Kowalke, *Kurt Weill in Europe*, Ann Arbor, University of Michigan Press, 1979, p. 465.
11 Bertolt Brecht reprinted in John Willett, *Brecht on Theatre*, London, 1964, p. 86.
12 Donald Mitchell, 'The Character of Lulu', *Music Review* 15, November 1954, p. 268.
13 Robin Holloway, 'The Complete *Lulu'*, *Tempo* 129, June 1979, p. 37.
14 *The Times*, 16 February 1981.
15 Robin Holloway, 'The Complete *Lulu'*, p. 37.
16 See George Perle, 'The Secret Programme of the 'Lyric Suite', *Musical Times* 118, August/September/October 1974 and Douglas Jarman, 'Alban Berg, Wilhelm Fliess and the Secret Programme of the Violin Concerto', *Newsletter of the International Alban Berg Society* 12, Fall/Winter, 1982.

17 Bertolt Brecht translated in Willett, *Brecht on Theatre*, p. 87.
18 *Ibid.*
19 George Perle, *'Lulu*: The Formal Design', *Journal of the American Musicological Society* 17/2 Summer, pp. 179ff.
20 George Steiner, 'Lulu: She is the Femme Fatale, the Man-Devouring Vamp', *The Listener*, 26 February 1981, pp. 265–8.
21 *Ibid.*, p. 266.
22 Tilly Wedekind, quoted in Leo Treitler, *Music and the Historical Imagination*, Harvard, Harvard University Press, 1989, p. 288.
23 See chapter 8, 'Wedekind and the Critics' in Elizabeth Boa, *The Sexual Circus*, Oxford, Blackwell, 1987, pp. 203ff.

Document 1: *Pandora's Box*

1 Kraus is primarily thinking of the strong German tradition of the domestic tragedy, which goes back to the eighteenth century with Lessing's two famous plays *Miss Sara Sampson* and *Emilia Galotti*. Goethe's *Faust* is also in his mind. But he is of course exaggerating his case.
2 *Maria Magdalena* is the title of a celebrated social drama (1844) by Friedrich Hebbel which turns on a father's refusal to accept, let alone forgive, the plight of his erring daughter. The father is a carpenter in a small provincial town; his daughter Klara is by implication identified with the Mary Magdalene of the New Testament.
3 The last two lines (not quoted) are as follows:
   Take heed, dear heart, of this large privilege;
   The hardest knife ill-used doth lose his edge.
4 Perhaps a reference to Wedekind's contemporary, Gerhart Hauptmann, some of whose major plays (e.g. *The Weavers*) are written in Silesian dialect.
5 Rebellious hero of Schiller's famous and influential "Sturm und Drang" play, *The Robbers* (1781).

Document 4: A note on Act III of *Lulu*

1 Vienna, Universal Edition, 1937.
2 'The Music of *Lulu*: A New Analysis', *JAMS* XII, 2–3, 1959.
3 Since this letter was not originally intended for publication, it contains several statements which were not as carefully formulated as they might otherwise have been. Scientific decorum suggests the following substitution for the above sentence: 'The appropriate scoring for an approximately equal additional number of bars may be inferred from the dramatic plan of III/2.' For this same reason, the words 'explicit' and 'exact' should be deleted from the two concluding sentences of the next paragraph, and further on, 'proof(s)' should read 'indication(s)'.
4 The references to Redlich's book are to the original German rather than the abbreviated English version.
5 Compare note 3.

6 Read: 'The third (final) Ensemble incorporates in their entirety the orchestral parts of the first and second Ensembles, from which the orchestration of more than 50 additional bars may be inferred.'
7 Compare note 3. The strictest possible interpretation still leaves 310 bars completely scored by Berg.
8 George Perle, 'The Cerha Edition', *Newsletter of the International Alban Berg Society* 8, Summer 1979, pp. 5–6.
9 George Perle, 'The "sketched-in" Vocal Quartet of "Lulu" Act III', *Newsletter of the International Alban Berg Society*, 12, Fall/Winter 1982, pp. 12–13.
10 See Friedrich Cerha, 'Some Further Notes on my realization of Act III of "Lulu"', *The Berg Companion* ed. Douglas Jarman, London, Macmillan, 1989, pp. 261–7.
11 George Perle, 'The Music of "Lulu": a new analysis', *Journal of the American Musicological Society* XII/2–3 Summer/Fall 1959, pp. 185ff.
12 Douglas Jarman, 'Lulu: the Sketches', *Newsletter of the International Alban Berg Society*, 6, June 1978, pp. 4ff.

Document 5: The 'lost' score of the *Symphonic Pieces* from *Lulu*

1 Hans Redlich, *Alban Berg: Versuch einer Würdigung*, Vienna: Universal Edition, 1957.
2 Rosemary Hilmar, *Katalog der Musikhandschriften, Schriften und Studien Alban Bergs im Fond Alban Berg und der weiteren handschriftlichen Quellen im Besitz der Österreichischen Nationalbibliothek*, Alban Berg Studien I, Vienna: Universal Edition, 1980.
3 Friedrich Cerha, *Arbeitsbericht zur Herstellung des 3. Akts der Oper 'Lulu' von Alban Berg*, Vienna: Universal Edition, 1979, pp. 7–8.
4 See Alban Berg, *Letters to his Wife*, trans. Bernard Grun, London: Faber and Faber, 1971, p. 421.
5 Berg made many other mistakes when writing the bar numbers into the full score of *Lulu*. The numbering of Act II, for example, is 100 bars out by the end of the act because he forgetfully added a hundred when turning over from p. 181 to p. 182 of the manuscript and converted the next bar number, which should have been 1040 into 1140.
6 I am indebted to George Perle for this information.
7 See Volker Scherliess, 'Briefe Alban Bergs aus der Entstehungseit der "Lulu,"' *Melos* 2 (March–April 1976): 108–14, for details of Berg's plans to compile a longer *Lulu* Symphony from the music of the opera. The passages at Act I, mm. 367ff., 515ff., and 526ff. at which the vibraphone part is cued into the piano part do not appear in the *Symphonic Pieces* but would have been included in the projected Symphony.

Bibliography

The following bibliography is confined to books and articles mentioned in the preceding text; it makes no attempt to be a comprehensive bibliography of the writings on either the Berg opera or the Wedekind plays.

Abraham, Gerald *A Hundred Years of Music*, 3rd edn, London, Duckworth, 1964

Adensamer, Eva 'Bergs geistige Umgebung – Briefe aus seinem Nachlass', *Alban Berg Symposion, Vienna 1980*: Alban Berg Studien II, Vienna, Universal Edition, 1981

Adorno, T. W. *Alban Berg: der Meister des kleinsten Übergangs*, Vienna, Universal Edition, 1968

Appleyard, Bryan *The Culture Club; Crisis in the Arts*, London, Faber and Faber, 1984

Berg, Alban *Letters to his Wife*, London, Faber and Faber, 1971

Boa, Elizabeth *The Sexual Circus*, Oxford, Blackwells, 1987

Boulez, Pierre *Orientations*, ed. Jean-Jacques Nattiez, trans. Martin Cooper, London, Faber and Faber, 1986

Brand, Julianne, Christopher Hailey and Donald Harris, *The Berg–Schoenberg Correspondence*, New York, Norton and Co., 1987

Cerha, Friedrich *Arbeitsbericht zur Herstellung des 3. Akts der Oper 'Lulu' von Alban Berg*, Vienna, Universal Edition, 1975

Drew, David 'Music Theatre in the Weimar Republic', *Proceedings of the Royal Musical Association 88*, 1968

Ewen, Frederic *Bertolt Brecht: His life, his Art and his Times*, London, Calder and Boyard, 1976

Gittleman, Robert *Frank Wedekind*, New York, Twaynes Inc., 1968

Hall, Patricia 'The Progress of a Method: Berg's Tone-Rows for *Lulu*' *Musical Quarterly 71.4*, 1985

Harris, Donald 'Berg and Miss Frida', *Alban Berg Symposion, Vienna 1980* Alban Berg Studien II, Vienna, Universal Edition, 1981

Hilmar, Rosemary *Kataloge der Handschriften, Schriften und Studien Alban Bergs . . . in Besitz der Österreichischen Nationalbibliothek*, Alban Berg Studien I, Vienna, Universal Edition, 1980

Holloway, Robin 'The Complete *Lulu*', *Tempo* 129, June 179

Jarman, Douglas *The Music of Alan Berg*, London, Faber and Faber, 1979
'Some Observations on Rhythm, Metre and Tempo in *Lulu*', *Alban Berg Symposion, Vienna 1980*, Alban Berg Studien II, Vienna, Universal Edition, 1981

'Friedrich's *Lulu*', *Newsletter of the International Alban Berg Society*, Summer 1981

'Weill and Berg: *Lulu* as Epic Opera', *A New Orpheus*, ed. Kim Kowalke, New Haven, Yale University Press, 1986

'Alban Berg, Wilhelm Fliess and the Secret Programme of the Violin Concerto', *Newsletter of the International Alban Berg Society* 12, Fall/Winter, 1982

Alban Berg: Wozzeck, Cambridge, Cambridge University Press, 1989

Kowalke, Kim *Kurt Weill in Europe*, Ann Arbor, University of Michigan Press, 1975

Krasner, Louis 'The Origins of the Berg Violin Concerto', *Alban Berg Symposion Vienna 1980*, Alban Berg Studien II, Vienna, Universal Edition, 1981

Lampert, Vera 'Schoenbergs, Bergs und Adornos Briefe an Sándor Jemnitz', *Studia Musicologica Academiae Scientarium Hungaricae* 13, 1974

Mann, Thomas *Diaries 1918–1939*, ed. Hermann Kesten, trs. Richard and Clara Winston, London, Robin Clark, 1984

Mitchell, Donald 'The Character of Lulu', *Music Review* 15, November 1954

Neumann, Karl 'Wedekind and Berg's *Lulu*', *Music Review* 35, February 1975

Perle, George '*Lulu*: The Formal Design', *Journal of the American Musicological Society* 17.2, 1964

'The Secret Programme of the "Lyric Suite"', *Musical Times* 118, August/September/October 1974

The Operas of Alban Berg, Vol. II; *Lulu*, Berkeley, University of California Press, 1985

'Some Thoughts on an Ideal Production of *Lulu*', *Journal of Musicology* 7.2, Spring 1989

Pisk, Paul A. 'Personal Recollections of Alban Berg', *Newsletter of the International Alban Berg Society* 10, Summer 1981, p. 21

Redlich, Hans *Alban Berg: Versuch einer Würdigung*, Vienna, Universal Edition, 1957

Alban Berg, London, John Calder, 1965

Reich, Willi 'Erich Kleiber an Alban Berg', *Schweizerische Musikzeitung* 98, 1952

Alban Berg, trans. Cornelius Cardew, London, Thames and Hudson, 1965

Russell, John *Erich Kleiber*, London, André Deutsch, 1957

Scherliess, Volker *Alban Berg*, Hamburg, Rowohlt Taschenbuch, 1975

'Alban Bergs analytische Tafeln zur Lulu-Reihe', *Die Musikforschung* 4, October–December 1977

Schoenberner, Franz *Confessions of a European Intellectual*, New York, Collier Books, 1975

Slonimsky, Nicholas *Music since 1900*, 4th edn, Cassell, London, 1971, p. 595

Steiner, George 'Lulu: She is the Femme Fatale, the Man-Devouring Vamp', *The Listener*, 26 February 1981

Szmolyan, Walter 'Helene Bergs Vermächtnis', *Österreichische Musikzeit-schrift* 32.4, April 1977

'Zum III. Akt von Alban Bergs *Lulu*', *Österreichische Musikzeitschrift* 32.9, September 1988

Treitler, Leo *Music and the Historical Imagination*, Cambridge (Mass.), Harvard University Press, 1989

Weill, Kurt *Ausgewählte Schriften*, ed. David Drew, Frankfurt, Suhrkamp Verlag, 1975

Willett, John *Brecht on Theatre*, London, Methuen, 1964

Wedekind, Frank *Gedichte und Chansons*, Frankfurt, Fischer Bücherei, 1968

Zweig, Stefan *The World of Yesterday*, London, Cassell, 1943

Discography

Of the two recordings of *Lulu* at present available only one, that by Pierre Boulez, includes Act III in Friedrich Cerha's completed version. The Dohnányi recording consists of only Acts I and II of the opera and the last two movements of the *Symphonic Pieces*. The famous recording by Karl Böhm with Evelyn Lear as Lulu and Dietrich Fischer-Dieskau as Dr Schön has now been withdrawn.

DG 2740 213
Conductor: Pierre Boulez
Cast: Teresa Stratas (Lulu), Yvonne Minton (Countess Geschwitz), Franz Mazuras (Dr Schön), Kenneth Riegel (Alwa), Toni Blankenheim (Schigolch), Gerd Nienstedt (Athlete), Hanna Schwarz (Schoolboy), Robert Tear (Painter), Helmut Pampuch (Prince/Manservant/Marquis)
Orchestra of the Paris Opera
(The final side of the recording consists of three talks on the opera by Friedrich Cerha, Pierre Boulez and Douglas Jarman.)
Recording released 1979

Decca D48 D3
Conductor: Christoph von Dohnányi
Cast: Anja Silja (Lulu), Brigitte Fassbaender (Countess Geschwitz), Walter Berry (Dr Schön), Josef Hopferweiser (Alwa), Hans Hotter (Schigolch), Kurt Moll (Athlete), Trudeliese Schmidt (Schoolboy), Horst Laubenthal (Painter)
Vienna Philharmonic Orchestra
Recording released 1978

Index

(Musical compositions and literary works apper under the name of the composer or author, but *Lulu* has a separate entry. References to newspaper, periodical or other bibliographical material is excluded.)